Yards and Stripes

Michael Francis

Copyright © 2020 Michael Francis
All rights reserved

Contents

Chapter 1 Sowing the Seed 1
Chapter 2 Four Meat Pies and a Snickers Bar 5
Chapter 3 Dog Wash 10
Chapter 4 Back to School 12
Chapter 5 On the Money 15
Chapter 6 Technical Difficulties 20
Chapter 7 Boston 23
Chapter 8 All Banks are Bastards 26
Chapter 9 Volkswagen 28
Chapter 10 A Lack of Local Knowledge 30
Chapter 11 The Launch 34
Chapter 12 My First Job 39
Chapter 13 On the Clock 42
Chapter 14 Hiding in Plain Sight 45
Chapter 15 What's in a Name? 48
Chapter 16 The Pintail Lane Chainsaw Massacre 52
Chapter 17 Lake Raisen 59
Chapter 18 A Happy Accident 64
Chapter 19 Riverside 67
Chapter 20 Don't Mention the War 72

Chapter 21	A Cup of Tea and a Tetanus Shot	74
Chapter 22	Qualifications	77
Chapter 23	Wisteria	82
Chapter 24	Squirrels	87
Chapter 25	An Offer I Couldn't Refuse	92
Chapter 26	The Trash Monster	97
Chapter 27	Anatomy	103
Chapter 28	Meet the Neighbors	109
Chapter 29	The Best Form of Defence	113
Chapter 30	The Greenwich Tsunami	118
Chapter 31	The Little House	122
Chapter 32	The Ultimate Upper Body Workout	125
Chapter 33	Moving On	131
Chapter 34	Marketing	136
Chapter 35	Well, It Seemed like a Good Idea at the Time	144
Chapter 36	Prospects	150
Chapter 37	The Clapboard Ridge Mole Invasion	152
Chapter 38	Off the Mark	157
Chapter 39	A Winter Exodus	160
Chapter 40	Overloaded	163
Chapter 41	Paving the Way	171
Chapter 42	Restructuring	176
Chapter 43	Back in Town	181
Chapter 44	The Big Day Out	185
Chapter 45	No Accounting for Taste	188
Chapter 46	Beaten and Shot	192
Chapter 47	Virginia	198
Chapter 48	The Last Chapter	201
A Note from the Author		207

CHAPTER 1

SOWING THE SEED

Fall, 2003

It was conceived as a grand adventure. Live in the United States for a few years and concentrate on what I had enjoyed doing most in my twenty-year advertising career. I would work as a copywriter with an advertising agency, while my wife furthered her legal career. Weekends would be spent drafting my novel, travelling across the country, and writing postcards home to the envy of family and friends.

That was the plan.

But the reality became working as an office temp, commuting from the New York City neighborhood of Jackson Heights, Queens, where I shared an apartment with Catherine and her partner Deborah. Catherine was from Wisconsin. She was pleasant, friendly, and worked as a teaching assistant. Deborah was from Brazil, she spoke broken English, and threw a decent left hook.

By that time, I was divorced, and it was my ex-wife who

alerted me to the Harry's Landscaping and Lawn Care franchise opportunity. She was working in the franchise department of a New York law firm, and dealing with a group of consultants who were in the process of establishing a platform for Harry's Group in the US.

I had heard of the business but knew nothing about it, until I was introduced to a fellow called Brian Dixon. Brian was the head of Hogan Franchising, and he explained that Harry's needed someone to launch its business concept in the US.

I thought it sounded like an exciting opportunity, and we arranged to meet the following week in the foyer of the Crowne Plaza hotel in Times Square. He drove in from Long Island. I took the dreaded 7 train, with its usual delays, and miraculously made it to the meeting on time.

We decided to go to a nearby coffee shop, and walked a few blocks past the hotel.

Brian opened his laptop and proceeded to explain the structure of the Harry's franchise model - a concept that had started with landscaping and lawn care and had since spawned nearly twenty different divisions. He focused very much on its middle tier investment opportunity. Or at least I did. I could become what he called a regional franchisor, a role that would allow me to secure exclusive rights to various Harry's divisions of my choice, within a specific geographic area. Thereafter, I would be free to operate my own franchise, while selling individual franchises to other people throughout my region.

Lawn care and to a lesser extent dog wash appealed to

me, and it certainly made sense to operate my own franchise. Doing so would provide me with an income and generate a degree of awareness. It might also establish a measure of credibility, as I figured if I could do it, anyone could.

I had absolutely no interest in gardening, had barely mowed a handful of lawns in my life, and I couldn't tell a weed from a wisteria. But hey, how hard could it be?

By the time my subway ride reached Queensboro Plaza, I had thoroughly mapped out my new business venture.

There was no point staying in New York. What I needed to do was live and work, in an upscale suburb where stockbrokers and CEOs made their cozy dwellings - in other words, Connecticut.

The next day I drove a car rental and headed north, making my way to New England. An hour later, I stumbled on the affluent commuter town of Greenwich. It had a quaint, almost English feel about it and was clearly an expensive place to live, given it had several high-end boutiques, countless hair salons, and a Rolls Royce dealership.

The town had no shortage of real estate agents, and over the next couple of weeks, I caught the train from Grand Central station a few times to do the rounds. I only wanted an apartment but would need a garage to store all of my equipment. The first agent I visited was Halstead, where "rentals are handled upstairs." I introduced myself to an impeccably dressed agent - a man who looked to be in his mid-thirties. I explained what I was looking for, my time frame, and other requirements.

"How much are you looking to spend?" he asked.

'Oh, I don't know. About seven, eight hundred a month.'

He looked at me as if I had just suggested he should marry his own sister.

"No good?" I asked meekly.

"We don't normally handle properties of that nature" he said.

Clearly not. Apparently, a decent apartment in Greenwich would set me back at least fifteen hundred dollars a month. Needless to say, I didn't stay long.

It seemed that agents such as Halstead concentrated more on the investment banker end of the market, with some even going so far as to adopt a "no rentals" policy - a kind of real estate apartheid.

I did, however, manage to find a more suitable agent. Cavendish Realty described itself as a rentals specialist. Their office was located just off Greenwich Avenue. "The Avenue" as the locals called it, was the town's "Main Street" and lined with designer shops, restaurants and art galleries.

My visit to Cavendish Realty was more productive, and I left with a copy of their listings for November.

I scanned the listings document on the train ride back to New York and once I got home, I booked a round-trip flight to Melbourne, to attend the regional franchisor training that was being held at the Harry's Group headquarters in Mornington.

Chapter 2

Four Meat Pies and a Snickers Bar

"This is Harry," the man said, explaining that I was the first US pioneer in Melbourne to attend the training course.

We shook hands, and I told him that I was looking forward to moving out of New York, working outside, and writing a book.

"You'll be too busy," he said.

I had no idea what the man was worth, but he owned Harry's Group, one of the world's biggest home services franchises. Not that you'd know it. He drove a 1981 Volvo, which had a coat hanger for an antenna, a chipped windscreen, and at least one bald tire.

Every preconception that I'd had of the man before meeting him was wrong. He was modest, unassuming, slightly built, and short.

Soon after, I was introduced to Greg O'Brien. He was in charge of the lawn care division. A former franchisee himself, he was very enthusiastic and physically imposing. Tall, dark, and heavy, he sported a thick bushy moustache and looked like Groucho Marx on steroids.

I had of course seen countless Harry's Landscaping and Lawn Care trailers on the streets of Melbourne. The business was clearly a great success, spreading throughout Australia and New Zealand, and it had all been started by one man with a lawn mower, a fistful of flyers, and an urgent need to pay the rent. Now Harry's was coming to the US, and I could be the first person to get on board - the first person to invest in the world's most successful home services franchise and in the biggest market it had entered to date.

It was all very exciting, and I was looking forward to exploring the more entrepreneurial aspects of the opportunity. But before I could, I was booked to spend two days working with Peter Bolton, a Harry's lawn care franchisee who operated in Melbourne's southern suburbs.

I arrived at Peter's home the following day, just before eight o'clock, and we were soon on the road to our first job. In fact, it was our only job, which may well sound like a rather soft induction, save for the fact we spent the entire day mowing lawns in and around a huge retirement village. We drove through and around the village, dropping off cans of fuel and empty grass sacks, as Peter's three employees were already hard at it.

Once we had completed a lap of the village, Peter pulled over and introduced me to the mighty Honda Buffalo, which for the most part was Harry's mower of choice. A brief safety introduction followed, before Peter stressed the importance of straight lines and neat edges. Then he let me loose on an unsuspecting nature strip.

There may be no great science to mowing a lawn, but at that moment, I was the very embodiment of focus and concentration. I dreaded making a mistake and feared running off the surface into the gutter, bashing the blades and planting what my colleagues called "donuts" in the lawn. Fortunately I managed to avert any such disaster, before I switched the machine off, emptied the catcher, and restarted, setting the throttle to the appropriate speed and the blades to a suitable height. I had passed the audition.

For the rest of the morning, Peter worked ahead of me, strimming edges, skirting around trees and garden beds while I followed with the Honda. He was soon out of sight, as I carried on at a steady pace, catching an occasional glimpse of the others who were all working at a frightening speed. No one had bothered to tell me we were taking part in some sort of speed mowing championship, and I began to feel that I was letting the team down with my careful, inexperienced maneuvering. I didn't dare rush for fear of making a mistake. Besides, I was already exhausted. Lunchtime couldn't come soon enough, and when the whistle finally blew, I limped to the nearest shop, where I demolished four meat pies and a Snickers bar.

I wasn't in any screaming hurry to get back to work and sat for a few minutes on a wooden bench by the side of the road. Already, I could feel my muscles stiffening. I could have taken Peter aside and said, "Thanks, mate, but I reckon I've got the gist of it," but I don't think that would have gone down too well at the office. Besides, who's to say that some other bloke wouldn't come over from the US and spend a day or two doing the same job? Well, I wasn't about to be shown up by some foreigner.

It was all the motivation I needed. I marched back, fired up the Honda, and set out to mow for my country!

I may have been forty, but I reckon at that stage of my life, I was about as fit as I'd ever been. I had been going to the gym regularly and swimming as often as I could. I was even keeping an eye on my diet. Still, when I woke up the next morning, I could barely move. It was all I could do to lift my head from the pillow. Clearly, all that time spent on a rowing machine at Planet Fitness, with a crazed Albanian personal trainer yelling, "Hudda! Hudda!" was scant preparation for hurling dozens of large sacks full of grass clippings into a trailer.

I didn't get up, so much as slid off the bed and on to the floor and then shuffled into the shower. Coffee, breakfast, and more coffee helped, but exactly how I managed to arrive at Peter's place on time remains a mystery.

Peter's employees were all going strong at the village, while we tended to a few other jobs. Actually, he tended to most of the jobs himself, while I listened and observed. Thank God for that.

We even had time to stop for lunch. It was interesting and enjoyable to just sit and chat. Not simply because we weren't working but because I was able to gather a picture of the Harry's organization and of the support it provided to franchisees, as well as the camaraderie that existed among them. I came to the conclusion that Harry's Landscaping and Lawn Care was as much about lifestyle as it was about income, and if the work didn't kill me, I was certainly going to save on a gym membership.

Chapter 3

Dog Wash

The second chapter of my induction involved spending a day with Gail Adams, a Harry's Dog Wash franchisee who lived in Eltham.

There were hundreds of Harry's Landscaping and Lawn Care trailers on the streets of Melbourne, and as distinctive and eye catching as they were, they looked like a station wagon from the seventies , alongside their dog wash cousins. The Harry's Dog Wash trailer was purposely built in fiberglass. It had its own tank with a rapid water heating element, a hydrobath, blow-dryer, interior lighting, a nonslip workbench, and an optional sound system. With its smooth lines and bright blue exterior, it looked like a scale model of the Space Shuttle. Well, it would have if the Space Shuttle was blue.

Our first client was a fat Labrador retriever in Hawthorn. Gail collected the client on a leash, led him on to the trailer and into the bath, as I stood watching over the rear "stable" door. She applied organic shampoo and conditioner, rinsing the client with warm water before lifting him onto the bench, where he was given a blow-dry, had his nails clipped, and was even perfumed. It was simply decadent. He was then returned to his owner. No doubt he felt like a new dog and I am willing to bet, that the minute he got home, he ran outside and rolled in a pile of compost.

Throughout the day, we clipped an Old English sheepdog and washed an array of breeds, including of all things a Siamese cat, which looked even more revolting and sinister when dripping wet.

The most interesting episode, however, came in response to a job that was sent in from the office. A client in Reservoir was the proud owner of two pit bull mutts, both of which needed a wash and worm treatment. I courageously waited next to the trailer, as Gail spoke to the client and collected each dog at the door.

"He keeps rubbin' and scratchin' his ass. It's drivin' him nuts," the woman said.

Sure sounded like a candidate for a worm treatment to me.

Gail led a powerful, ugly, and downright nasty looking dog on to the trailer. It looked like a pit bull crossed with a pit bull as far as I could see, and I was only too happy to give my friend all the space and time she needed. The wash, dry, and treatment passed without incident, and Satan was soon returned to his owner. Then Gail led Osama on to the trailer. I didn't dare look inside, for fear that direct eye contact might instigate some sort of canine homicidal tendencies, but to be fair, both dogs behaved perfectly well throughout.

Of course I knew they would.

Chapter 4

Back to School

The following Monday was the first day of Harry's School - regional franchisor training at the office. The first person I saw that day was Greg O'Brien. He asked me what I had learned during my few days on the road.

"Well, I'm not as fit as I thought I was," I said. Greg smiled like he knew.

The highlight of the morning was without doubt Harry himself. The face that launched a thousand trailers, spoke quietly and modestly for the best part of an hour. He explained the organization's motto and wrote it in large letters on the white board: "FIND AND KEEP THE BEST PEOPLE." Rather prophetically, he had accidentally used a permanent marker, leaving a clear imprint of the words on the board all week, long after the scent of ink and solvent had dispersed.

We broke for lunch, and I was able to chat for a while with the man himself. I told him about Greenwich and that initially I was just hoping to generate enough work to survive.

"Don't worry about getting the work," he said. "There's plenty of work. You need to find really good people as franchisees."

In retrospect, I wish I'd had the presence of mind to have asked him, "And just how do I do that?" After all, he had more than a thousand franchisees himself, so he should've known, but alas, I was distracted by the arrival of the sandwiches.

Over the next few days, we covered territory rights, business reviews, advertising, marketing, branding, research, and communication. Then we did a role-playing exercise. We were split up into groups of three, and I was teamed up with a roofer and one of the cleaners. Two of us sat back to back, simulating a telephone conversation, while the third would be critiquing our performance. We were each given a script, outlining our own specific circumstances, and we were asked to play different roles. I was cast as a franchisor, calling the roofer on the phone. He was behind in paying his fees and he hadn't returned calls or attended meetings. In three minutes, I was supposed to address the situation as best I could, then the cleaner would report to the class and give me a score out of ten.

I raised all of the relevant issues in the script but failed to get the roofer to agree to a payment plan or give a commitment to attend future meetings. The cleaner's critique was reasonably kind, before the roofer chimed in.

"Michael's a really nice bloke," he told the class. "In fact, he's too nice."

Greg then wrote the words "too nice" next to my name on the white board.

Oh, the shame.

Chapter 5

On the Money

I was dressed appropriately for a sunny February afternoon in Melbourne - shorts and a polo shirt - yet quite absurdly for a cold, wet, and miserable morning in New York.

Naturally, the flight from Australia to the US was long, but it was rendered more so by the fact that the Qantas movie schedule was absolute rubbish. I was reduced to watching *The Fighting Temptations*," if only to appreciate the fact that Beyonce couldn't act to save her life, but to my lasting disappointment, she was actually quite good.

Later, I entertained myself by collecting as many bread rolls as I could from the flight attendants and hiding them under my tray. I ate most of them between meals but kept three of similar proportions to juggle outside the toilets.

We stopped in Hawaii before landing at JFK, where someone cornered me in the baggage claim, asking where I had bought my boots.

"Australia. Bit of a hike from here," I said. "Cheaper though."

I took the AirTrain from JFK to Jamaica and the subway to the Brooklyn neighborhood of Williamsburg, where it was pissing down, as Americans say. Dragging a suitcase and wearing a pair of shorts was no way to tackle weather like this, but I needed to pick up a key to a friend's house, where I had arranged to stay, so I decided to hail a cab.

Once in Williamsburg, I dried off and stayed a few days, before moving to more permanent temporary digs in Hempstead, Long Island. My friend Alexis was living alone in a two-bedroom apartment. She was moving back to Australia in a month and was grateful for a bit of extra rent.

It was a situation that suited me perfectly. I could come and go as I pleased, and although I was a bit far from Greenwich, I was able to travel there by train and reacquaint myself with the rental market.

I even secured a one-month trial membership at the gym, which I discovered had rowing machines with a programmable pace boat on the monitor. No need for a crazed Albanian here! After some instruction, I was able to set a time and mile rate, which allowed me to effectively race against an oval-shaped silhouette. I became quite engrossed in the "contest," providing my own radio style commentary, complete with special comments - sometimes, I fear, out loud.

I caught the Long Island Rail Road to 34th Street and then took the subway to Grand Central station, where I hopped on Metro-North to finally take me to Greenwich. I sat on the train, secure in the knowledge that I would have to come up with the equivalent to the GDP of a small

African nation for a security deposit on the apartment I'd finally end up renting.

The fact that I had insisted on a garage with a lock limited my options, but I did manage to find a studio apartment in the Central Greenwich neighborhood. It was unfurnished but, by local standards, reasonably priced at $1,200 per month. I dealt with an agent, told some outrageous lies as to my income, forged some employer references, and insisted on curtains. The landlord asked for a twelve-month lease, six weeks rent as a deposit, with a month in advance. In the end, we settled on $1,100 and a month's deposit, which I dare say covered the cost of the curtains.

I arranged to move in toward the end of March and spoke to my "Man with a Van," a Turkish tournament chess player called Mr. Ugur.

While I was away, I had managed to store all my belongings in a small museum in Manhattan, where I had occasionally worked during my temping career. It meant retrieving everything at night after the museum had closed, and we set about lowering my queen-size mattress and box spring from the library's roof. It was a difficult enough exercise getting them up there in the first place, but the reverse was something else entirely. For a time, it seemed to be a question of whether we would crash through the ceiling and subsequently demolish the gift shop or vice versa. Thank goodness for Mr. Ugur. His use of straps, ropes, ladders, and ramps rendered a minor miracle.

"Mr. Michael. We are on the money!" Mr. Ugur proclaimed.

It was an expression I had used back in December and one he had since adopted as his own. We were "on the money" when we had lowered everything down, and once again, when it was loaded onto the van. We were also "on the money" as we drove out of New York, reached the New England Thruway, found the Greenwich exit, and finally arrived at the apartment.

I was beginning to wish he didn't speak English.

We lugged everything up the stairs and sat for a moment by the window of an otherwise empty living room.

"Mr. Michael, you want sofa bed?"

Well yes, I thought, before Mr. Ugur told me about a very comfortable, almost brand-new sofa bed that I could have for free. All I had to do was help him move some furniture for his friend. I agreed and spent an entire day the following week loading furniture on and off his van, before I was rewarded with a tattered, stained, mustard-colored monstrosity with one missing leg. No sooner was it sitting in the living room when I decided to take it to the trash.

Back at Lex's place, I did the rounds of the ShopRite supermarket and Dollar Tree store, managing to accumulate enough plates, glasses, and cutlery, to ensure I wouldn't have to wash up more than once a week. It was far too much to carry on the train and Lex didn't own a car, so I called a friend who did. Ailsa was a colleague from my New York temping career who lived in Brentwood, Long Island, and drove an SUV.

We could have picked a better night. It was cold, drizzling, and very foggy. It was all we could do to pick out the taillights of the car in front of us, and the only signs that were clearly visible were the ones hanging over the highway with lit-up letters that read "Fog." They were about as useful as those that flash "Delays Ahead" when you are stuck in traffic.

Fortunately, the weather eventually cleared, and as we were approaching the apartment, Ailsa asked me about my new neighbors. I explained that I had only met a couple, since I'd just moved in recently, but so far, they seemed very nice.

Ailsa then drove her car into the parking lot at the rear of the building, and I was able to see through a window into one of the first-floor apartments. There, presented for the world to see, was a free-standing laundry rack, complete with an array of socks and underwear that had no doubt been basking in the sunlight earlier in the day.

"Oh but fair dinkum," I said. "Have a look at this bloke, will you? I mean honestly mate, do you really think we want to sit around all day looking at your bloody jocks and socks?"

Before I could protest any further, I felt obliged to offer a retraction.

"Oh, hang on a minute." I said. "That's my place."

Thankfully, no notes of complaint had been slipped under the door, and I made a mental note to consider the various angles that made my apartment's interior visible to others, lest I display my laundry so brazenly again.

Chapter 6

Technical Difficulties

Established in my new abode, the next task was to set up an office. I arranged to have the phone connected, and before long, my "Welcome to Verizon" package arrived in the mail. I followed the instructions to the letter, installing the software for the modem and putting all the plugs in all the right places. The lights were on, but when it came to accessing my email, no one was home. I rang the Verizon help desk, and together with the customer service rep, we spent an age reinstalling the modem and altering various settings on my computer, delving into the bowels of the hard drive to places I never even knew existed. Nothing worked. The line was testing okay, and we had tried everything short of taking it out to dinner.

There was nothing more we could do. Verizon would have to send a technician out, a process that took several weeks. When the tech finally did arrive, he tested and monitored the modem, the cables, the phone, and all the connections. They were all fine. It wasn't until he went into the living room that he was able to identify the problem. It seemed that a previous resident had a cable TV connection, since there was a socket set against the wall with two outlets. I had connected the modem to a socket beneath the tiny graphic that looked to me like a computer screen. It was of course supposed to represent a television. The socket, an inch to its left (the one with the unmistakable telephone graphic), that is where I was supposed to plug the cable in. After several phone calls, hours of adjustment, and weeks of waiting, the Verizon tech was able to fix the problem in less than a second.

Of course it's easy when you know how.

He was kind enough to wait while I connected to the Internet. Unfortunately, in the process of trying to fix the original problem, I had completely disabled the anti-virus software, firewalls, and basically every security setting there was. As soon as I connected, my computer was quite literally hijacked. I sat dumbfounded looking at the screen, as some unseen force took total control. Countless pages of unknown origin and dubious content flashed before my eyes. No doubt the virus floodgates had been thrown open, and soon the entire operating system seized up. I was surprised there wasn't any smoke billowing from the back of the machine.

"Isn't the Internet fantastic?" he said.

The next day, I caught a train to Bridgeport, carrying my crippled laptop to the closest computer repair shop I could find. I did my best to explain what had happened and basically blamed Verizon for the whole mess. The bloke behind the counter took charge of the patient and wrote a very detailed, technical memo: "Reinstall anti-virus. Clean up shit on hard drive."

Chapter 7

Boston

Even without email access, I was able to make the necessary arrangements to attend the upcoming International Franchise Exhibition, and of course, no prizes for guessing that yours truly would be manning the Harry's booth.

The exhibition ran for two days at the Boston Convention Center. Hundreds of franchise businesses had been booked in a massive hall, where all manner of companies had set up elaborate displays, in order to impress and cajole prospective franchisees. We hadn't. The Harry's booth was barely three yards square and consisted of a backdrop with a massive "Harry's Group" sign, surrounded by logos for each individual division. Apart from that, there was a small table, a stool, and me, wearing a Harry's Landscaping and Lawn Care shirt.

It was a difficult two days. No one in the US had ever heard of us, and I didn't know much more than the people attending the exhibition. Every now and then, someone would stop and say, "Tell me about Harry's Group." I did my best to explain how large and diverse the business was and that I was the first (in fact only) person to come on board in the US. I also mentioned that I was establishing my own Landscaping and Lawn Care franchise in Connecticut and that I hoped to develop the Dog Wash division as well.

"So why should I buy a franchise from you then?" someone asked.

Now I was really stuck. I had rehearsed the general corporate profile piece well enough, but I hadn't given a lot of thought to answering what was (let's face it), a pretty obvious question. I think it's fair to say my first few contacts left largely unconvinced, but it wasn't long before I was in for a real shock.

A bloke from New Jersey came by, looked me squarely in the eye, and all but demanded to know about Harry's. He was assertive to the point of being aggressive, and no sooner had I trotted out the bit about my own lawn care franchise, he interrupted, "You'd better put some neat stripes on those lawns, boy."

"Stripes?" I asked.

He looked baffled. "Of course. Plenty of rich people in Greenwich. They will all want stripes on their lawn."

"Whaddya mean stripes?" I repeated.

He threw his head back and laughed out loud. "You are starting a lawn mowing business in Greenwich, and you don't know how to put stripes on a lawn?"

The fact is I had no idea. The answer could have been "with a brush" for all I knew.

"Oh well," I said. "Perhaps I'll just concentrate on the

Dog Wash business." That was the most polite way I could think of saying bugger off. It failed.

"Tell me about the Dog Wash then?" he demanded.

Clearly, this bloke wasn't going anywhere. He was having the time of his life, watching me clutch at every metaphorical straw I could find. Just for a moment though, I thought I had him, as I waxed lyrical about the trailer - water tank, rapid heating element, blow-dryer, nonslip bench, stylish exterior, fiberglass. It felt like I was landing a painful blow with each jab.

"What do you do with the waste water then?' he asked.

Damn. I thought for a moment. "Well, you just let it out in the street."

He did that thing with his head again. "You can't just let it out in the street!" he bellowed. "The Environmental Protection Agency will come down on you like a ton of bricks. They'll fine you thousands!" He walked away and yelled out after a few steps, "Good luck, buddy."

I doubt he meant it.

The rest of the exhibition was largely uneventful, as I spent most of the time perched on a stool, racking my brain as to how on earth you put stripes on a lawn.

Chapter 8

All Banks are Bastards

I caught a train to Bridgeport the following week and picked up my laptop. It was working again, but the hijack episode had clearly done irreparable damage. It was now painfully slow to complete even the simplest task and consequently, it came dangerously close to doubling as a Frisbee, but for the time being, it would have to do. A new computer was a luxury I couldn't afford, since I had to finance a new vehicle, buy all my equipment, and keep the nearby Chinese takeout in business.

I had been banking with Bank of America, but I only had a personal account and an Australian credit card. If I wanted to open a corporate account, I would have to make an appointment. I called in to a nearby branch and asked to speak with the manager, explaining that I wanted to open a corporate account and discuss financing a vehicle. I was given someone's name and an appointment for later that week. I then went home to look over my business plan.

I returned a few days later and met with my contact.

Although I introduced myself, the introduction wasn't reciprocated. To this day, I can't be sure if she was even the person I was supposed to meet with, since she didn't bother telling me her name or giving me a business card. All the same, I assumed it was okay to sit down, since she already had.

I slid my business plan across the desk, explaining why I was there and what I hoped to achieve. Jane Doe typed my details into a computer as I spoke. It wasn't a long meeting. I had only been a resident in the United States for a short time, and since I was operating a start-up business, there was really nothing she could do for me.

"We have to do what the computer says," she said.

I had flown back and forth across the globe, been badgered half to death at the recent franchise exhibition, and moved into an expensive apartment in Greenwich. Not to mention the fact I had prepared a comprehensive business plan, and now I couldn't even open an account. I tried to explain all of this, while my contact looked at me with a combination of disinterest and impatience.

"We used to be able to consider things like that" she said, "but these days, we just have to do what the computer says."

I left her office, walked home, and composed a detailed letter of complaint about the bank's procedures. I then logged on to Bank of America's website and posted my complaint on their customer feedback page. I'm still waiting for a reply.

Chapter 9

Volkswagen

The attitude I encountered at the bank was disheartening, but when I was at the Harry's headquarters in Melbourne, Greg O'Brien had told me how helpful and generous Volkswagen (Australia) had been in developing a purpose-built Harry's Landscaping and Lawn Care vehicle. The idea was to house a lockable box on the back of a Volkswagen Transporter cab chassis, rather than tow a trailer. I was even there when a bloke from Volkswagen handed the keys to Harry, later posing for photos and telling him he could pay for that one down the track once he sold it on.

I could hardly wait to meet with the Volkswagen people in the US. Were they ever going to be excited about Harry's! Here was a business with twelve hundred individual franchisees in Australia, entering a market ten times the size. We could have a thousand franchisees operating in the US within five years. That's a thousand new vehicles, and I was the catalyst. These people were going to treat me like royalty. I was looking forward to days out in corporate boxes at

Madison Square Garden and Yankee Stadium. They might even give me a vehicle for free, just to get the ball rolling. I may have hit a bit of a snag at the bank, but Volkswagen was going to be all over me like a cheap suit.

I couldn't have been more wrong.

I met with two representatives of Volkswagen Commercial Vehicles and tried to explain the potential that I believed Harry's had in the US. I presented figures that showed the growth of the business throughout Australia and New Zealand. I projected similar success in the United States, and suggested that Volkswagen could both supply and finance each vehicle. I explained it was imperative that we get the first one on the road as quickly as possible and the importance of service and follow-up.

I handed them a CD that contained all the specifications for "the box," foolishly accepted their quote as "inclusive of a substantial discount," and gave them an order right then and there. Little did I know that it would be the best part of four months before they would deliver.

Chapter 10

A Lack of Local Knowledge

The acquisition of a branded Harry's vehicle was crucial, not just in operating my own business but also in order to recruit franchisees throughout New England. I had invested in an iconic (albeit Australian) brand, and I wasn't about to advertise, let alone present the concept, to a potential franchisee without one. Even so, I couldn't afford to wait for Volkswagen or the banks to join the party and I decided the only way to get the business going and pay the rent, was to throw myself into my new venture.

Peter Bolton and I had been exchanging emails, and he had given me an equipment wish list. With my recently acquired Internet access, I set about finding a local supplier and Googled "lawn mower Greenwich, Connecticut." My search directed me to a retailer on the outskirts of New Canaan.

The next day, I walked to the Enterprise rental outlet on Edgewood Avenue and hired a van. Armed with my New England road atlas, I then managed to undertake an estimated forty-minute drive across the state, in the best part of two hours - the US highway system is very unforgiving.

Chief Equipment was more of an agricultural supplier, judging by the fact my mid-sized van was dwarfed in the company of various John Deere tractors and assorted farm machinery. I asked to speak with whoever was in charge and was introduced to the sales manager. I explained my situation and confessed the fact that I had gotten lost driving from Greenwich.

'Greenwich?' he asked, looking surprised. "Why didn't you just go to SiteOne?"

He told me that SiteOne was the biggest garden and landscaping supplier in the region and would definitely have everything I was likely to need. What's more it was only a forty minute drive away, given the SiteOne showroom was located within walking distance of my apartment.

Suffice it to say, I felt like a fool, but the exercise wasn't a complete waste of time, as I discovered that one puts stripes on a lawn by using a mower that's equipped with a roller.

Embarrassed and admonished, I drove back to Greenwich and returned the van.

The next morning, I set out on foot for King Street, where SiteOne was located and within twenty minutes, I was walking through their showroom. Dozens of lawn mowers stood on the showroom floor, while numerous shovels, forks, and assorted gardening implements adorned various display stands.

Chris Martin was the manager. He was very helpful, courteous, and wore a tie, which I thought was rather extravagant for someone who sold lawn mowers, but he seemed to know what he was talking about, judging by the fact he was across the whole roller mower stripes thing. I explained what I hoped to achieve with Harry's Landscaping and Lawn Care, and Chris assured me that SiteOne could supply all of our franchisees with everything that they would ever need, starting with me.

The first order of business was a lawn mower. SiteOne stocked a range of Hondas, but the Buffalo wasn't among them. In fact, all the mowers in the US were configured differently to those in Australia. For one thing, most incorporated a self-propulsion system, and all of them had a blade brake mechanism. My "friend" from the franchise exhibition had convinced me that the residents of Greenwich would insist that their lawns be adorned with stripes, so I settled on a Honda mower with a nineteen-inch deck and a roller.

What I knew as a Whipper Snipper masqueraded in the US as a String Trimmer. In any case, Chris recommended a Stihl model that featured a bump feed head for the cord, one that could be interchanged with a blade or an adjustable hedge trimming attachment. I was assured that this was indeed the best model on the market, notwithstanding the fact that Stihl, was clearly a German word meaning "hard to start."

A leaf blower was added to the list, as were rakes, a spade, a shovel, and a fork, before we approached the health and safety aspects of the job and added ear defenders and safety goggles. I was happy to follow Chris's advice as he included spare mower blades, engine oil, and a set of spanners, in the unlikely event I would ever actually undertake any equipment maintenance.

    I didn't have a bank account yet, at least not for the business, but handed over the Visa card and arranged delivery.

Chapter 11

The Launch

Having made the commitment to buy all the necessary equipment and feeling secure in the knowledge that my friends from Volkswagen would do everything possible to provide me with a vehicle, I formulated my marketing strategy. I decided to launch my business by means of distributing flyers, so I emailed my friend Russell in Melbourne, asking him to design one for me. Other than my uniform, Harry's didn't have any brand presence in the US, but I had to start somewhere.

I asked Russell to place the Harry's logo at the top of a flyer and to feature a list of services and my telephone number.

"We" offered the residents of Greenwich a prompt, reliable, and personal service for all their lawn care and landscaping needs, and suggested they call "us" for lawn mowing (which I had done for a couple of days in Melbourne), hedge trimming (which I had done once for about five minutes), rubbish removal (something you don't exactly need a degree for), gutters cleared (refer to previous), pruning and lopping (actually it's probably better you call someone else for that, given there is some chance they may actually know what they're doing) and general maintenance (whatever that means).

I claimed that most jobs could be done the same day, boasted a full money-back guarantee, offered free no-obligation quotes, and set about finding a printer.

Google had spectacularly failed to locate one of the biggest lawn mower retailers in the area, so I decided to deploy a more primitive means of research and flicked through a copy of the yellow pages.

Lakeside Printing was located across the street from the station. It was a ten-minute walk from my place and about a hundred miles from the nearest lake. Happily, they were more adept at printing than geography, and before long, I was handed one thousand two-color flyers, with Harry's Landscaping and Lawn Care prominent in dark green type.

By this time, all my new toys (I mean equipment) were safely housed in my garage, but short of pushing and carrying them between jobs, I had no means of transport. Needless to say, I called my friends at Volkswagen. I spoke to one of the people with whom I had met previously - a fleet sales specialist no less. He told me that since I'd been a US resident for less than three years, Volkswagen would not be able to provide a finance package. They would be only too happy to build and supply, but I would have to buy the vehicle outright or secure finance with one of the banks (not Bank of America presumably).

I was absolutely staggered and told him as much. From my perspective, I alone would launch the biggest garden and landscaping franchise in the world into the largest market it had yet entered. For all I could see, Harry's was presenting Volkswagen with the opportunity of a lifetime - the opportunity to supply vehicles to every franchisee in the US, which given there were already twelve hundred in Australia, could conceivably number in excess of two thousand within five or ten years. Surely, even for a company as substantial as Volkswagen, that was a serious slice of business.

My pitch fell on deaf ears.

It was a very frustrating situation, but I decided the best way forward was to establish a relationship with a bank that could see the "bigger picture" and go from there. After all, surely not all of the banks in a country as large and diverse as the United States would be as obstinate and difficult as Bank of America. Perhaps not all, but Chase, Wells Fargo, Capital One, and Citibank certainly were, as I discovered the "three-year rule" wasn't the exclusive domain of Volkswagen and Bank of America. I contacted my bank in Australia and suggested that I secure some sort of finance package from them, but since mine was "a start-up business overseas" - well, you can guess the rest.

I was embarrassed to find myself in this predicament and having secured the rights to Harry's Landscaping, Lawn Care, and Dog Wash for all of New England on a strict commercial basis, I was reluctant to ask anyone with whom I had dealt with to date for any help. Eventually, I decided to share my frustration with some of the senior people at

Harry's Group, only to learn they were collectively involved in a significant "rethink" with regard to the whole US operation. In fact, the managing director and operations manager thought so long and hard that they chose to resign (effective immediately), while Brian Dixon and Hogan Franchising were unceremoniously sacked, amid a plethora of email saber rattling, and threats of legal action.

It seemed to me as if Harry himself had filed the entire US venture in the "Too Hard Basket." Even so, I had a thousand flyers and a garage full of equipment. Rather than sit around and worry about the situation, I set about making some sort of an impression myself. I donned my hat, laced up a pair of running shoes, and hit the streets of Greenwich.

I walked up several streets in my neighborhood. There wasn't a single house that had a mailbox on the street. It must be a statutory requirement in Connecticut that letters are delivered through the front door, which wherever possible should be at the end of a long, steep driveway. I was well aware that most of my flyers would have a shelf life that could be measured in seconds, which made it all the more frustrating to think I was walking up to half a mile at a time to adorn a kitchen trash can liner.

As I walked down Anderson Road, I saw an elderly man tackling the lawn on a steep gradient in front of his house. He was standing about ten feet above street level and propelling a hover mower attached to a rope, down what was surely quite a dangerous slope - at least from his perspective anyway. He had measured the distance by wrapping the rope around his wrist and was effectively cutting the grass each time he hauled the machine back up the slope. He was wearing a short sleeve button down shirt, tailored shorts, dark socks that reached halfway up his shins, and brown leather, lace-up shoes.

I walked up the driveway and offered him a flyer.

"No thank you," he said, clearly focused on the task at hand.

I was convinced he was in the process of killing himself, and all but pleaded with him to let me help. I offered to mow his lawns for free, but he was having none of it.

"Go away please. I'm busy!" he shouted, as the mower descended once again.

I left flyers for his neighbors and every other house on the left, then turned around and repeated the process on the other side of the street. Twenty minutes later, I saw the old man was still at it. There was no point giving him a flyer, I should have offered him a job.

Over the course of the next two days, I delivered about six hundred flyers, each of which featured my home telephone number with a 203 area code, since several people had told me it was important that I be perceived as a local business owner.

God forbid anyone might think I lived in New Haven.

Chapter 12

My First Job

Mr. Creesey was the first to call. He was a retired gentleman who had twenty-three grandchildren. His house was on Locust Street and I can only assume he concluded that my willingness to undertake odd jobs extended to happily risking my life, as a section of his roof had collapsed. I'm very uncomfortable with heights at the best of times, and even though my entire roofing knowledge could be inscribed on the head of a small pin, I made an appointment for 2:00 p.m.

I arrived to find Mr. Cressey standing in his front yard. A pair of binoculars hung around his neck. He was staring at the remnants of several broken tiles that had once formed the apex of a roof, which sat above three stories. I introduced myself and assessed the task at hand in as much time as it took to turn on a tap. I didn't even own a ladder, let alone a crane, and wondered if my entire venture could be any more unsuccessful than if I were to crash to earth from a height of a hundred feet while tackling my very first job. We agreed it was a task that should be undertaken by a specialist contractor and that given he "kept himself fit" mowing his own lawn, there was (for the time being at least), nothing I could do for him. He liked my hat though.

I didn't have long to wait for my next opportunity, when I retrieved a phone message from Jo Breen. Of course, if I had remembered to transfer my incoming calls to my cell phone, I could've saved myself the trouble of walking home before returning to the very same street - but there's no point in commiserating.

Jo was the mother of two young boys; she was friendly, attractive, and made the best coffee in Greenwich. She was American and the coffee Italian.

I continued to mow Jo's lawns every two weeks, until her father retired and proved to be cheaper than me. I was treated to a mug of coffee each time and often cheered on by her two sons who would be peering through a window and over the back of the couch. I once offered to prune her privet hedge and was paid without question in spite of the fact that I did a pretty ordinary job and it grew back in less than a month. One day, I shattered a window in her new sunroom by flicking a pebble with the strimmer, yet she managed to convince the builders it was somehow their fault, rather than let me pay for it.

If all my clients were as lovely as Jo, I may still be mowing lawns.

The first time I did a job for her, I arrived in a beat-up, old van that I had hired from Enterprise. The second time I did a job for her (two weeks later), I arrived in a beat-up, yet otherwise new, Volkswagen van. In the course of two weeks, I had managed to back it up into a brick wall, hit a tree, and sideswipe a concrete barrier in a supermarket parking lot.

It pretty much looked like any other white van, save for the fact it was adorned with an enormous VW logo on both sides, with the words Volkswagen Commercial Vehicles in large letters underneath. Anyone stuck behind me in traffic could not possibly escape the fact that they could "hire this van for $75 a day!" Huge orange and yellow letters made certain of that.

My next lead came from a house on Lenox Drive. Clare Murray needed someone to trim the conifer hedge that bordered the driveway, and to clear out the gutters of her two-story house. I wasn't really equipped, much less insured to work at the heights required, but my detailed risk assessment concluded that the chance of suffering a serious physical injury was far outweighed by the fact that Clare had all the attributes of a supermodel, so I happily agreed to tackle both jobs.

I trimmed the hedge as best I could and was genuinely surprised when she complimented the work I had done.

"It looks fantastic!" Clare said.

"Does it? You are kidding?" I replied, stepping in front of the worst of the misshapen sections.

Chapter 13

On the Clock

Even without a branded vehicle, it was abundantly clear to all when I was working in the vicinity. I dare say the rhythmic scream of the Stihl Kombi System could be heard in neighboring towns. I imagine it was the noise that attracted Clare's neighbor, a woman who effectively owned the other half of the hedge that divided their two driveways. She inspected and, to my surprise, complimented the job I had done trimming the Murray's hedge, and she asked if I could tackle her side and the top. She accepted my quote, and I set about the task, finding my confidence with the hedge trimmer growing at much the same rate as the discomfort and pain in my shoulders. All the same, she was happy with the job and asked if I might undertake a few other things for her.

Quoting jobs was one of the most difficult aspects of being a "Harry," and I found myself a bit on edge when trying to provide an estimate for the various tasks my new client had in mind. I was to clear away a rotten pile of compost from behind a garden shed, remove a satellite dish attached to the side of the house, demolish a stone firewood holder, dismantle a number of kitchen cabinets, pull up several yards of carpet, and spend an hour or two introducing her two sons to games of "Backyard Cricket." Although to be fair, I was happy enough to throw in the last bit.

I had no idea how long it would all take, and in the process, I ignored Harry's First Commandment: "Thou shalt not provide an hourly rate." We settled on twenty-five dollars before I set about dragging several yards of stinking compost into a dumpster.

Over the course of the next week, I came and went between other jobs. I unbolted the satellite dish, dismantled the kitchen cabinets, ripped up the carpet, and tried any number of times to deliver a "leg break" with a tennis ball to a young boy holding a baseball bat.

A trip to SiteOne added a sledgehammer to my equipment collection, which I wielded with some purpose against the concrete firewood holder at the side of the house, all the while finding it oddly empowering to systematically demolish something.

I was conscious of the fact that I was working by the hour and made sure I didn't waste any time in getting the various jobs done. Needless to say, the meter wasn't running for games in the backyard, but when I totaled everything up, it came out to sixteen hours at $25 or $450. I was surprised how much time had "added up" and was a little concerned that my client might feel the same way, so as a gesture of goodwill, I amended the total to $375.

She wasn't unhappy with the invoice, so much as raging mad and quite frighteningly unreasonable. In short, she refused to pay and all but accused me of being a thief. In response to my politely written reminders, I received a letter from her lawyers. I called her and suggested she pay whatever she thought was a fair amount and we could leave it at that.

A few days later, I received another lawyer's letter. I never recovered a cent, decided to put the whole ordeal down as a lesson learned, and some months later, took great delight in the fact that a fallen tree had demolished much of her front fence.

Chapter 14

Hiding in Plain Sight

The flyers that I'd been delivering were starting to pay off, and I was fielding an increasing number of jobs. One such call came from Mrs. Fishwick, who lived at "Mallards" on Lawrence Street. I made an appointment to look over her property, and she gave me a detailed set of directions - "Eighth house on the right-hand side from the corner of Lexington Avenue." Number 36 would have done just as well.

"Mallards" was a two-story house that had lawns at both the front and back of the property, a shed, a greenhouse, a pond, a slope, a playground along with a trampoline, and two massive willow trees that had deposited countless twigs, leaves, and sticks on the grass. From a lawn mowing perspective, it was like a military assault course.

Undeterred, I quoted thirty dollars to strim the edges and mow the lawns, and another twenty to clear away all the weeds that were growing around the pond. I maneuvered the strimmer around the swings, trees, and trampoline, deciding to mash through the twigs and sticks with the mower. Once I finished, the lawns looked quite good, so I then set about demolishing the sea of weeds that surrounded the pond. There was an abundance of them. Light green in color and at least a couple of feet high. No worries, I thought, as I waded among them in a pair of shorts. The effect was almost immediate, as I felt a sharp, scratchy, almost burning sensation. I tried to ignore it and busily swung the strimmer from side to side, hacking down great swathes of the offensive growth, but soon, I was forced to retreat. I leapt back, dropping the strimmer on the ground, furiously raking my fingers over my legs, oblivious to the fact that my hands and arms were brushing against the very same menace that was already torturing my flesh. I had no idea what was happening. One minute I'm strimming a perfectly harmless bunch of weeds, and the next, I'm trying to literally tear my skin off. It was as painful as it was bizarre.

I tried everything I could to ease the discomfort - rubbing, scratching, swearing, but it only made things worse. I rolled in a garden bed, ran my legs under a tap, and smothered myself with grass clippings. None of it made the slightest difference. It was agonizing, but I soldiered on, finished the job, and shoved an invoice through the door.

I then rushed to a drug store on Greenwich Avenue and worried that they wouldn't take my symptoms seriously, I described everything in great detail. I needn't have bothered. Apparently, I had encountered stinging nettles, a relatively common feature of the local landscape and the horticultural equivalent of the box jellyfish.

I would have happily paid that pharmacist a thousand dollars to alleviate the agony. As it so happened, I parted with about five, which was probably just as well, since the creams and lotions that I liberally applied didn't make the slightest difference. I went home, hopped in and out of the bath (which only made things worse) and paced back and forth, completing countless laps of my apartment, throughout an entirely sleepless night.

Chapter 15

What's in a Name?

Fortunately, the symptoms started to subside the next day, and I ventured out to quote another mowing job. This one was on Millbank Avenue.

Mr. Vaudrey was an older, very nice man. His house (like most on the street), was absolutely huge and built on a large block of land. It went without saying, that he needed someone to mow the lawn. I thought the job was worth forty dollars, but I quoted him thirty. Still, he seemed quite shocked.

"Goodness me. That's rather a lot. Mr. Clark used to do it for twelve."

"Twelve dollars?" I said in disbelief, surveying the back garden, which was the size of Yankee Stadium. "You're kidding?"

"No. Twelve dollars," he assured me.

It was a job, that even with a riding mower, could not possibly be completed in less than an hour, which given the fact I would have to collect and dispose of all the clippings as well, made twelve dollars an absurdity. However, it begged the question: "Just where is this Mr. Clark, and why isn't he doing it now?"

"He can't do it. He's in hospital," Mr. Vaudrey said. "He's got pneumonia."

I said that I wasn't the least bit surprised, and soon after, we settled on thirty dollars. I completed the job and then we chatted over a cup of coffee before he referred me to a neighbor who owned an even bigger property and was in a similar bind. It came as no surprise that Mrs. Forbes-Hamilton (not her real name) was also a client of Mr. Clark. On this occasion, I was out of sync forty-five dollars to sixteen, a prospect that she could simply not entertain.

"I can't possibly pay that," she protested.

"I can't possibly do the job for any less," I replied.

"Well, what on earth am I supposed to do then?" she demanded.

I suggested she move into an apartment. It was a remark she either didn't hear or simply chose to ignore, since to my astonishment she told me to go ahead.

Two hours later, I finished the job, gratefully accepted her check, and accordingly, designated Millbank Avenue "Off-Limits."

My next call came from Mrs. Martin who lived on Mallard Drive. Her property was called "Ashbury," which could be found on the left-hand side of the street after turning right from Anderson Road, just beyond the second speed bump. I followed her directions to the letter and discovered that "Ashbury" was also the house with a large number 8 attached to it.

Meeting Mrs. Martin was like being introduced to the mother of one of your friends from school. She was pleasant and friendly with a confident, assertive manner. Her previous gardener had "moved on," and she was anxious for me to spend an hour and a half there every couple of weeks, mowing the lawn and doing various bits and pieces. There wasn't much grass to mow, and the rear of the property was on a steep slope, but I was encouraged by the fact that if we scheduled the job for Thursday mornings, she would rarely be home and could leave instructions with her house cleaner. I thought twenty-five dollars per visit was too cheap but agreed all the same. I mean you don't argue with your friend's mom!

Dealing with Mrs. Martin worked out quite well. Her house cleaner was indeed always there and armed with a set of written instructions. I spent some of the time mowing but most of it weeding garden beds, raking up leaves, and cleaning out gutters. More importantly, however, I could always count on a cup of coffee.

It wasn't long before I managed to attract the attention of the neighbors. Mrs. Cole lived opposite Ashbury and the next-door neighbor was Sally Ann Bolt. Both became regular mowing clients, which meant I could now complete three jobs without having to move the van. Mrs. Martin's twenty-five dollars wasn't such a bad deal after all.

Mrs. Cole's property was flat and relatively easy to mow, although after I had butchered the edges of her lawn with the strimmer, she insisted I use her own set of shears instead

- a minor blow to my professional pride. Sally Ann's property was, by contrast, every bit as steep as Mount Ashbury. The back garden was two tiered, which meant lugging the mower up a long set of wooden steps to a kind of base camp, before making a final assault on the summit.

By this point, I was starting to build a healthy client base and making some new friends along the way. The weather had been quite good, but I was still driving around in a rental van, I didn't have a business bank account, and above all, I had no idea as to what was happening with the whole Harry's foray into the US.

CHAPTER 16

THE PINTAIL LANE
CHAINSAW MASSACRE

I had by now all but given up on financing a vehicle through Volkswagen, and every bank that I had approached wasn't the least bit interested in dealing with me. I thought perhaps if I spoke to an accountant I might, at the very least, be able to solicit some advice. I was referred to a local firm called Roberts and Green. I called their office and was introduced to one of the partners. After explaining my situation, I was given an appointment for later that week.

Bob Lawrence and I met over a cup of coffee in an Italian bistro on Greenwich Avenue, which was across the street from his office and definitely a less formal surrounding. I explained how I came to be presented with the Harry's franchise opportunity and how huge and diverse the business was in Australia - to say nothing of my own lofty ambitions for my corner of the US. Bob listened, took notes, and gave me the impression he was genuinely interested, which, in and of itself, was encouraging and something of a revelation. I shared my frustration of dealing with banks and how important it was that I finance a vehicle. He said I shouldn't worry and that he would speak to a contact of his at Bank of America. All the same, I wasn't holding my breath. We then shook hands and went our separate ways.

The following week, I had my second appointment with Bank of America. This time I managed to reach the top floor, where I met with Bob's contact. Jeremy Thompson had spent his entire working life with the bank and was a matter of weeks away from a well-earned retirement. Clearly, ours wasn't going to be a long-term relationship, but the mere fact I was sipping coffee in his office was a pretty good start.

The age-old adage as to who, rather than what you know, certainly rang true that day. I don't know what Bob had told him, but the bloke couldn't do enough for me. I probably spent less time in that office than I did when meeting with any other bank. The difference was that this time I left, not with a burning sense of frustration, but with a new business account and a vehicle finance agreement.

Thanks to Bob, things were looking up. I walked down Greenwich Avenue and called the people at Volkswagen, telling them to get a move on. Then I listened to a couple of voicemails, which promised some more work.

The first message was from Lisa Pullen, who had retrieved one of my flyers from her mailbox on Pintail Lane. Lisa was a slim, attractive mother of two young children. True to the Greenwich stereotype, she drove a massive SUV-as you do, when you have to negotiate a couple of speed bumps on the way to the shops.

Lisa gave me the impression of someone with too much time on her hands. She employed a full-time nanny and seemed to have no shortage of ideas as to what to do next with the house and garden. For one thing, she appeared to have a local builder on some sort of retainer. As she and I strolled around the garden together, it was clear she had some ambitious plans. As to whether or not I (with all of six weeks' experience) was the best person to be carrying them out, well that was another matter.

The first task I undertook was to help her builder dismantle, reassemble, and relocate a wooden garden shed. I think we moved it all of four feet. Next up, I was to clear away a mass of tangled shrubs and small trees growing in a corner of the property, so as to make way for the installation of some elaborate monkey bars for her children. Some of the branches and trunks were quite thick and beyond the capacity of my existing tool ensemble, which could mean only one thing - chainsaw. It was an exciting prospect and one I fairly leapt at. I had never used a chainsaw before, and oblivious to the fact that I was as likely to sever a limb as a branch, I went shopping.

I arrived at Lisa's house the following morning, and soon after, I made a detour to SiteOne, where I had purchased a brand-new Stihl model the previous day. I stood on the shop floor, resplendent in my Harry's uniform, thinking that I had never seen the showroom so crowded. It was fairly brimming with customers - residents of Greenwich and its surrounding towns, all potential clients and advocates of Harry's Landscaping and Lawn Care. At least, that was until Manager Chris Martin spotted me and called out, "What? Can't you start it?!"

As embarrassing as it was for a garden and landscaping "professional," there was no disguising the fact. My brow was fairly dripping with perspiration, my cheeks were flushed, and my hair was disheveled. I was holding a brand-new chainsaw in my left hand, as my right arm had entered some kind of spasm, having tugged countless times at the rip cord in a vain attempt to start the motor.

"No," I replied sheepishly.

Chris kept me waiting while he served a customer. A process I have no doubt he extended for comic effect, as he could barely contain himself when he approached and ushered me outside. We stood in the parking lot, and I handed the chainsaw over, insisting it was faulty. Chris put it on the ground, braced it with his foot, and adjusted the choke. He tugged three times on the rip cord, concluded that the motor was flooded and then all of a sudden, amid great palls of smoke and the stifling odor of gasoline, he had the audacity to start the damn thing.

He revved the throttle a few times (as if to labor the point), sending the chain spinning around the bar at the speed of light - all the while alerting everyone within a five-mile radius, to the fact that he had single-handedly saved the day. Show off.

Chris explained the role of the choke (as if I was six years old) and gave me a crash course in the nuances of the Stihl

MS 230, before I drove back to Pintail Lane with a renewed sense of purpose.

I carried the chainsaw into the garden, placed it on the ground, and braced it with my foot, just as Chris had done. I switched the choke a third of the way on, tugged twice on the cord and then turned the choke off. I prayed silently and tugged again.

The MS 230 roared into life.

Revving it triumphantly, I adjusted my safety goggles and ear defenders, before crawling beneath the prickly branches of a sturdy holly tree, ripping through its trunk like a hot knife through butter. I found it quite thrilling, as I went to work on its secondary trunk, the one sprouting from the turf a few inches to the right.

To this day, I wish I had taken note of the fact that the bark on the trunk - which I thought was from the same tree - was clearly different from the original. It was smooth by comparison and lighter in color, but it wasn't until I dragged it from the tangled mess that I realized my mistake. As I pulled the base of the trunk toward me, I looked across and aghast when a colorful mass of lilac disappeared into a sea of dark green.

My new chainsaw had been in operation for less than two minutes, and even though I was still physically intact, in the blink of an eye, I had managed to ruthlessly execute Lisa Pullen's fifteen-year-old rhododendron.

I thought it was desperately unfair that the base of a plant was anchored at least six feet from where its foliage actually protruded. I think that's what the legal profession would deem "contributory negligence." All the same, it was the one thing in the entire project that Lisa had specifically asked me to protect, or at the very least, retain.

I hauled the evidence across the lawn, dropped it on the ground, and started piling the other cuttings on top of it, in a desperate and futile attempt to conceal my crime. I thought perhaps if I took the visual element out of the equation, Lisa might be so enthralled by the exciting expanse I had created, that she might forget she ever had a perfectly healthy plant growing there in the first place - like that was going to work.

I had the presence of mind to switch the chainsaw off, when I saw her walking toward me. In the event she decided to attack me with it, I figured I could probably cover about three blocks before she got it started.

I really should have owned up and taken full responsibility, but to my everlasting shame, I chose to "play dumb." My flimsy, awful defense was that I didn't realize she hadn't wanted the tree murdered in the first place. In any case, I suggested that my "scorched earth policy," would afford her two children even more room to play and that consequently, they would grow up to be even stronger, healthier, and more rounded human beings than they otherwise might. It was a kind of "big picture" scenario.

I was amazed and relieved when she reacted in an almost Zen-like manner. She didn't scream and she didn't cry. In fact, she didn't even raise her voice. She appeared quite calm and philosophical. Just moments earlier, I was convinced that my Harry's career was over. Now it was as if the governor had telephoned, granting a full pardon, just as the executioner was about to flick the switch. I could have kissed her, but instead I simply cleared away all of the rubbish, cleaned up the site, and moved on to my next adventure.

Chapter 17

Lake Raisen

Mr. Raisen lived at the top end of Lincoln Avenue. He had seen my advertisement in the *Greenwich Sentinel* and thought perhaps I "could have a look at doing a few jobs around the garden."

He sounded like an ideal client - friendly, getting on a bit in years, and lived quite close by.

We arranged to meet, and I arrived at his house at the appointed time. There was a car in the driveway, but when I rang the bell and knocked on the door, there was no answer. I was wary of proceeding any further, lest I discover that Mr. Raisen bred a particularly aggressive strain of Doberman, but given the small wooden gate (a few feet to my right), was hanging off its hinges and held together by a frail piece of twine, I came to the conclusion that was unlikely to be the case.

I opened the gate, placed it back on its hinge, fixed the twine, and strolled around to the side of the house, walking past a sunroom that looked out over the garden. I stood in the open doorway, where I could clearly see two people inside - Mr. and Mrs. Raisen no doubt. They were both smartly dressed and fast asleep. Not wanting to induce a heart attack, let alone two. I coughed, cleared my throat, and walked back to the front door, trying to make relatively polite, but discernible, noises as I went. I knocked on the door again but to no avail.

I walked back to the sunroom to see them both still slouched in their respective armchairs.

I wondered if perhaps they had died simultaneously - a harmless, elderly couple, done in by the shock of a particularly spiteful editorial on Fox News.

Fortunately, that proved not to be the case, since after I had spent the best part of fifteen minutes belting the living daylights out of his front door, Mr. Raisen finally opened it.

"Ah. Harry's Landscaping!" he said excitedly.

"Yes, Mr. Raisen. How are you?"

He shook my hand and looked at his watch. It was a quarter past three.

"Sorry I'm late" I said.

He stepped outside, ushered me through the gate and toward the sunroom, where he introduced me to his wife (now wide awake), who also reminded me of the fact that I was "late." I apologized and made a mental note to invest in a megaphone.

Mr. Raisen, whose sports jacket, tie, and trousers contrasted with my scruffy shorts and boots, took me on a tour of the garden.

He escorted me on to a lawn that resembled the 15th at

Augusta. It was an expansive, undulating fairway, complemented by a water hazard. He called it a pond. It looked more like a lake to me.

In any case, he and his wife had long enjoyed the fact that migrating wild ducks would nest there for a couple of months in the fall. The ducks hadn't turned up for a few years, apparently due to the plethora of weeds that now clogged the water. A close inspection revealed that a mass of thick, dark-colored weeds were indeed thriving - so much so, that there was barely a patch of water that wasn't affected. I could only imagine what it looked like from the air. The weeds themselves were suspended beneath the surface. They weren't actually anchored to anything, let alone rooted to the bottom, and as such, it was relatively easy to drag them out with a rake. Mind you, there were a lot of them.

My mission was to wade in and clear out as many as I could. Given the weather had been quite warm, it was a job that appealed as a kind of final act refresher. I could mow lawns, trim hedges, weed, and rake throughout the day, then spend an hour or so waist-deep in cold water. I offered to come twice a week in the evenings, for as long as it took. Mr. Raisen agreed and we struck a deal.

I had spent much of the time while we were walking in the garden doing some mental arithmetic, calculating a quote to mow the lawn. It was a big enough job for me and surely beyond a man of my client's advanced years, but to my surprise, it was the one task he was determined to complete himself. Instead, he gave me a long list of things to do, which included digging over the rose garden, clearing out the borders, and painting all the gutters at the front of the house.

I offered to tackle the rose garden then and there. Firstly, because it didn't look to be a particularly big job, and secondly, because when Mr. Raisen had asked me to "clear out the borders," he'd made it quite clear that I should leave all of the heather intact. Given I had no idea which plants were in fact "heather," I put that task to one side, until I could find a visual reference on the Internet.

The rose garden itself was arranged in a circle, set inside some paving stones that were just outside the sunroom. I fetched a fork and spade from the van, and set about making short work of all the weeds and a few dead stems.

With Mrs. Raisen looming over me as an interested spectator, I thrust the fork into the soil with some gusto, causing it to rebound with enough force to jar my shoulder and almost break my wrist. I dropped the tool, grabbed hold of my arm, and recalling the fact that my elderly client was within ten feet, I exclaimed, "Goodness. That's a bit firm!" Needless to say, "firm" wasn't the first four-letter word that sprang to mind.

It was a hard lesson. I had given the Raisens a fixed and modest quote to dig the garden over, thinking it would take less than an hour. What I hadn't realized was that the soil was so dry and compressed that it was like concrete, and probably the reason why all of the roses had long since died in the first place.

I had no option other than to continue, though it was a painfully slow job, which wasn't helped by Mrs. Raisen's constant supervision (from the comfort of the sunroom), as I scraped, clawed, and bashed for the next three hours. Eventually, I managed to clear every weed and each dead rose, then I called it a day, went home and fell asleep in front of the TV.

Chapter 18

A Happy Accident

The next morning, I met Mrs. Birt, a new client who lived across the street and down the hill from Jo Breen. Her house was located at the top of a steep, narrow driveway, and her garden was a bit of a mess. The lawn was long, and patchy and low branches hung over the driveway, making its borders resemble a tropical jungle. There was enough work to keep me busy for months, but Mrs. Birt only wanted me to come once every two weeks for a few hours at a time.

I had hoped to stick to the principle of giving a fixed quote for each specific job, but given that strategy had failed miserably the previous day, I agreed to an hourly rate and offered to start immediately.

My first task was to clear the garden beds of weeds and other undesirables. Mrs. Birt pointed to a number of plants and reeled off a few Latin names of the species she "obviously" wanted to protect. None of them were all that "obvious" to me, so I suggested that if she could tell me which ones were in fact the weeds, I would happily pull them out. She laughed for a moment but then realized that I was in fact serious, so she gathered a fistful of clothespins and Post-it notes and attached them to the plants that I should leave alone. Although it was an embarrassing admission to make, I wasn't about to masquerade as an expert - not after the "Pintail Lane Chainsaw Massacre" anyway.

Finally, she left me to get on with it, and I worked fast and hard. Before long, I had a huge pile of waste in the back of the van and had made a discernible difference, to one side of the driveway at least. I was quite proud of the job I had done, but above all, she was happy - so much so that she asked me to tackle the lawn at the back of the house and clear away some weeds from around the pond.

The back lawn was quite flat but punctuated with obstacles like swings and pet enclosures. I set about strimming the edges and parts of the lawn that the mower couldn't reach, quite oblivious to the fact that I must have absolutely terrorized the two guinea pigs taking refuge in their hutch.

I made a good job of the lawn and was looking forward to actually completing a project without any discernible drama, when I set about weeding the rocky border to the pond.

It was small, and there weren't even that many weeds, but access to them was tricky, since some of the rocks were loose and slippery. I had pulled out all but one, when I made the mistake of reaching across the water to complete the final act. It wouldn't have taken any great effort to simply walk around to the other side, but to my great misfortune, I chose to lean across, placing the toe of my boot on a wooden trellis that stretched across the pond itself, resting just above the water level. A sliver of pine gave way and my foot plunged in, causing me to lose my balance and fall forward. I executed a spectacular belly flop as I crashed into the pond, destroying the trellis (probably squashing a couple of the goldfish) and getting drenched in the process.

I wasn't hurt, but I clearly had some explaining to do. I gathered the broken pieces of the trellis, tossed them and all of my equipment in the back of the van, and headed over to the house. Given the fact that I was dripping wet, I could have probably spared my client much of the detail as to exactly what had happened, but I gave her a full account of the incident, together with an apology.

As it so happened, she was well aware of just how rotten and fragile the trellis was. She had placed it there several years before when her children were much younger - presumably a safety measure in the event one of them was foolish enough to fall in. In any case, she'd wanted to get rid of it for some time, and I had in fact done her a favor.

"No worries," I said. "Any time."

Chapter 19

Riverside

I was steadily building a solid base of clients, but from both a practical and marketing perspective, it was imperative that I had my proper Harry's Landscaping and Lawn Care vehicle on the road. I called my contacts at Volkswagen to check on the progress and was assured everything was "under control" and that I could expect it in a couple of weeks. I was particularly anxious because a potential franchisee in Connecticut had contacted me, and I didn't particularly fancy turning up for a meeting in a rental van.

In the meantime, I had an appointment to meet with a new client that morning. Her name was Nicola Gill, and she lived in Riverside - a neighborhood of Greenwich that was bordered on three sides by water: the Mianus River, the Cos Cob Harbor, and the Long Island Sound.

She had two jobs in mind for me. The first of which was mowing the lawn. In the past, she'd had an arrangement with a local bloke, who did a few people's lawns for some extra cash, but he had recently bought a new car and his wife wouldn't let him put the mower in the back. The second job was a bit more involved, and it required a site inspection of "the shed."

Nicola's shed was located in the far back corner of the property. As far as I could see, the overall structure was solid and sound, but the roof was absolutely shot to bits. It was full of holes, rotted through in places, and in the process of collapsing - a process that I managed to accelerate (to my cost), by poking a particularly damp section with a broom handle while standing directly underneath. Mind you, the roof itself (what was left of it anyway), was nothing more than sheets of particle board, covered with supposedly waterproof roofing felt.

Nicola wanted the roof replaced. She and her husband had put their house on the market, and a neat, practical, intact garden shed was only going to add to the home's value. By the same token, she didn't particularly want to spend a lot of money getting it fixed, so I proposed demolishing what was left of the roof and replacing it with sheets of particle board, covered with supposedly waterproof roofing felt.

I didn't dare climb on the roof itself, as I didn't particularly fancy the prospect of being a human wrecking ball, so I did my best to measure the task from ground level. I made a few notes, drew a diagram, and took everything to a local hardware store.

It wasn't long before the old roof was no more, and I was soon piling damp, rotten piles of mush into the back of the van and replacing them with brand new sheets of particle board.

It wasn't until I was fitting the third and fourth sheets that I hit a bit of a snag.

I had carefully measured the overall dimensions of the roof, but what I hadn't taken into account was the distance between each of the joists that I was laying the sheets across. The first row overlapped by a few inches, which was all well and good, but the second would be lying over just the one, and only a couple of inches from its edge at that. Ultimately, it might look all right to the eye, but woe betide anyone who had occasion to walk on the roof, as I for one wouldn't be taking the short odds it would hold.

I thought of pulling up the first row of sheets and sawing them off so that they could effectively share the same joist but trashed that idea, when I realized I would be wasting a lot of material and subsequently buying more.

With the first two sheets nailed down, I lifted up each subsequent one, laying them over the joists, trying various combinations and arrangements in search of the most secure and cost-effective option, much like a giant Tetris puzzle. It was quite an exercise to maneuver such large sheets into different positions and having squashed a couple of fingers in the process, I came to the conclusion that it was, after all, only a shed. I reverted to my original design, and once I had all the sheets in place, I found that only two of seven rows were perhaps not as secure as I would've liked. Even so, I still had to get up on the roof to nail them all down, a process I undertook with the utmost care.

Attaching the felt would present more of a challenge.

I had bought three large, six-foot wide rolls and each of

them was very heavy. I climbed up a ladder, lifted the first roll onto the roof, and set myself to rolling it all the way across in one fell swoop - a distance just shy of eight yards.

Perched on a middle rung of the ladder, with my waist level with the roof, I rocked back and forth a couple of times, as a means of building momentum, and heaved as hard as I could.

It rolled about a foot.

I reached over, drew it back, and tried again, but with a similar outcome.

The felt was so thick and so heavy that it would only roll a few inches at a time, so I resorted to using a "beached whale" technique in order to roll it out. I lay face down on the roof, trying to spread my weight across as large an area as possible, nudging and pushing each roll a little bit at a time. I dare say I looked quite silly, not that anyone could see me, but the fact was I was too scared to care in any case. I was constantly worried that my next shove might be my last and that at any moment I would come crashing through the roof and into the shed, where I'd be impaled on a rusty garden tool.

By now it was getting quite late, but I was determined to finish the job, lest the wind slip under the roofing felt overnight, deposit it all on the ground, and undo much of my hard work. I crawled and wriggled across the roof, tapping a hammer as I went, trying to sound out the joists. I emptied an entire packet of tacks, and secure in the knowledge that the roofing felt wasn't going anywhere, I climbed down, stood back, and admired my work.

I thought it looked like a first-class job and told myself so.

Mind you, it was quite dark at the time.

Chapter 20

Don't Mention the War

The next day, I had an appointment in Stamford, Connecticut's second largest city and home to Yale University. My client was Mrs. Franklin, an elderly English widow who had been married for many years to a famous artist - someone I was clearly expected to have heard of. She was a painter herself. Although she wasn't as good as her late husband (by her own admission), she continued to conduct workshops and training courses under his name.

She lived in a large two-story house, set amid what was once a gorgeous and picturesque garden. No doubt it had proven to be a source of inspiration in both her late husband's and her own paintings. But sadly, it had long since become overgrown and was now littered with nettles, brambles, and all manner of horticultural nasties.

Though quite frail, Mrs. Franklin was a cantankerous character, who complained time and again that other gardeners she had employed would turn up once and never return. The latest culprits were "two young men from the golf club" who had promised they would come every two weeks. I felt sure that she had simply scared them off, but even so, it wouldn't have come as a great shock if one day their remains were discovered hidden in her cellar - their demise a result of being drugged, and hacked to death with their own tools.

Giving Mrs. Franklin a quote was always an adventure. After arriving, I would wait by the door while she located her walking stick. She would then escort me to a particular section of the garden and explain exactly what she wanted me to do. Then I would give her a quote. She in turn would reel back in horror, insist that I must have made a mistake, and go on to complain about how much things had gone up since the war. We would then move on to another part of the garden, repeat the exercise, and so on.

Unlike my predecessors, I did return, and over time, I managed to clear all of the overgrown paths, so that she could at least stroll around the garden. She even extended an invitation to an exhibit featuring some of her work and that of her many students. She was genuinely surprised and seemed quite thrilled when I showed up, taking me by the hand and conducting a private tour.

Most of the works were for sale, and I was handed a price list.

After perusing it, I too was shocked as to just how much things had gone up since the war.

Chapter 21

A Cup of Tea and a Tetanus Shot

I started the day by ringing Volkswagen, and after suffering through a detailed account of my contact's weekend at the beach, I was asked (not for the first time) to confirm that the dimensions of the purpose-built box and the angle of the mower ramp on the vehicle were in fact okay. Given I had handed the same bloke a set of detailed specifications and drawings (several weeks before), it was clear to me that his question was merely a tactic to justify the fact that delivery would be further delayed. There was little more I could do, so I hung up the phone, loaded the rental van and set off to see a new client who had responded to my ad in the local paper.

Mrs. Stigger was in her nineties and lived with her daughter in Riverside. She was a very friendly, gentle woman with whom I probably spent as much time drinking tea and eating cookies, as I did mowing her lawn.

Befitting someone with her gentle nature, Mrs. Stigger had a habit of adopting rescue dogs - animals that had often been neglected and abused in the past. She would have two or three living with her at any one time, which presented its own set of challenges when it came to looking after the lawn.

Let's just say I soon learned to keep my mouth shut when using the strimmer.

I arrived to mow the lawns one day, well aware that Mrs. Stigger had recently made the difficult decision to have one of her aging and arthritic border collies put to sleep. What I didn't realize is that she had managed to replace it (almost immediately), with a tortured psychotic. Without a doubt, the ugliest and most evil dog I had ever seen - a powerful, thick-set mongrel with a dull, matted coat and bright yellow eyes.

We first met, when I quite innocently opened a gate leading to the back garden. A split second later, its jaws were wrapped around my leg and its teeth were buried in my flesh. I had no idea how it may have been treated in the past, and at this point, I didn't much care. I was just grateful for the fact that it responded and recoiled, after being repeatedly punched in the head.

The dog let go, just long enough for me to leap back, cry out in pain, and pull the gate shut.

Mrs. Stigger had heard the commotion from the kitchen. She had come outside and ushered the dog in. We then carried on a rather perverse conversation. Each of us was on either side of the gate, where she did her best to assure me that everything was perfectly fine and where I did my best to explain to her that I was in fact bleeding quite profusely.

Eventually, I was granted leave to visit the Greenwich

Hospital and assured that a cup of tea would be waiting for me upon my return.

A tetanus shot, some antiseptic, and a few stitches later, I was back in business and attending to my regular clients as if nothing had happened, although I did put off my evening dip in "Lake Raisen" for a week.

Chapter 22

Qualifications

By now, existing clients were referring me to some of their friends and relatives, which was certainly encouraging. One such referral introduced me to a man who lived in Norwalk, which was a bit of a drive north.

Mr. Taylor owned a small property that backed on to a forest. His front and back lawns were immaculate and the gardens well-kept. At first glance, I didn't see much work for me, given that he was clearly capable of doing a good job himself. That combined with the fact that he seemed to regard me with a degree of suspicion.

We stood in his back garden. With his arms folded, Mr. Taylor asked me to no end, questions about Harry's Landscaping. I trotted out the well-rehearsed corporate history but stumbled when it came to my own qualifications and experience. He was curious to know the attributes I was looking for in a franchisee. I didn't think for a moment that he was interested himself, but thought perhaps he might know someone who was, so I explained that practical skills and experience counted for little.

"Communication and the ability to deal with people are paramount," I said. "Anyone can learn how to mow a lawn, but you can't teach someone to be honest, reliable, and hardworking."

He seemed surprised to learn that I wasn't necessarily aiming to recruit qualified gardeners and that there really wasn't much of a horticultural aspect involved in our initial training. Even so, he said he was looking for someone to commit to a weekly schedule of maintenance, alternating lawn mowing with weeding and general tidying of the garden beds. I explained that I was more comfortable giving him a quote for a specific job than providing any sort of hourly or half-day rate, but I managed to dodge the issue by assuring him that I would check my schedule and mail a written quote to him. He accepted the arrangement and then presented me with the details of a specific job that I could perhaps undertake for him.

The branches of a number of trees were growing over the fence that bordered the rear of his property, and he needed someone capable and qualified in the use of a chainsaw to sever them. Consequently, he would then have a supply of firewood for the winter. It sounded like an ideal opportunity. There was no confusion as to which tree or branch to saw, and all I had to do was follow the line of the fence, lop off the branches, cut, and stack. Easy.

"No doubt, you've got your TCIA?" Mr. Taylor asked.

I confessed that I had no idea what he was talking about.

"Your arborist license," he said. "You aren't allowed to

do any work for hire on trees in Connecticut without it."

"Well I have," I said.

He made it quite clear that under no circumstances should I be doing any kind of work on trees, let along using a chainsaw without a license. I suggested that he must be mistaken, as I had in fact purchased a chainsaw recently, although to be fair to the people at SiteOne, I had told them that I had used one several times before, which was of course completely untrue. Mr. Taylor stood his ground, adamant that he was in the right.

I then asked him how it was that he knew so much about arborist qualifications anyway.

At this point, I had of course ignored the long-standing legal precedent of never asking a question that you don't already know the answer to. As it happened, Mr. Taylor had recently retired from his position as chairman of the Connecticut Tree Protective Association or CTPA.

I sent him a letter the next day, outlining a schedule of work and costs to maintain his lawns and garden. He wrote back, thanked me for my time but politely declined my offer. I can't imagine why.

That evening I had an appointment to meet Tom Harker - my very first franchise prospect. I showered, changed, and arrived at the Long Ridge Tavern in Stamford, wearing a Harry's polo shirt. I met Tom in the bar, and we sat down over a couple of beers. He had come from work and was dressed in jeans and a shirt splattered with paint and plaster.

After being laid off from a stock brokerage firm in Hartford, he had been renovating a couple of houses and was considering a franchise investment. Whatever he decided to do in the future, it was clear that after an eight-year stint as a stockbroker, a return to the corporate world didn't particularly appeal to him.

I explained how it was that I had come across the franchise opportunity and that being from Melbourne, I couldn't help but be aware of the tremendous success that Harry's had become. Aware that I had no real experience of the Harry's franchise system, to say nothing of the fact that I had arrived in a van emblazoned with "Volkswagen Commercial Vehicles," I stressed the fact that it was "early days for us in the United States" and tried to focus the conversation on what I knew of the operation in Australia.

It was clear that Tom had been doing his research. I was impressed with how much he knew of Harry's, if a little disappointed to learn that he was on the verge of signing a franchise agreement with a lawn treatment company.

The US franchise market was awash with lawn treatment opportunities. I had seen plenty of other lawn care and garden maintenance franchises in Australia, yet none that offered a specific lawn treatment service. Oddly enough, the reverse was true in this part of the world. As far as I could see, lawn treatment amounted to spreading fertilizer on clients' lawns throughout the course of a year. It wasn't particularly physical or varied, but perhaps that was the appeal. I couldn't knock it, as any lawn treatment franchise that I could name (and there were several) was already bigger, longer established, and dare I say, more successful than I was.

Tom explained his territory structure and outlined his ambition to have a multi vehicle operation within five years. It was a difficult pitch to counter, given he appeared committed, focused, and seemed to have a more clearly defined business plan than I did. I really didn't have a shot to fire, so we had another beer, talked about other things, and agreed to keep in touch.

Later that night, I sat down in front of the computer, and after checking the latest AFL news, I read an email from Jason Johnson.

Jason was an experienced Harry's franchisee and a regional franchisor in Melbourne. He had been involved with the company almost from its inception and had recently been appointed by Harry to effectively re-launch the business in the US. It was the first bit of news that I had received in weeks and a clear indication that perhaps the US operation hadn't been forgotten about after all.

Jason had decided to make a fact-finding trip to the US in a few weeks and he had already booked a flight. It was an exciting prospect, and with the knowledge and experience he would undoubtedly bring, perhaps his trip would be exactly what the business needed. I replied to his email, said I was delighted that he was coming over, offered to pick him up from the airport, and extended an invitation to stay in my apartment.

Chapter 23

Wisteria

It took four months, several meetings, and numerous phone calls, but my custom-built Harry's Landscaping and Lawn Care vehicle finally arrived. I was relieved to see that it did in fact adhere to the specifications I had supplied. Everything that was supposed to open and shut did. There was a ramp that folded down for the mower, it had shelved units along the side, and a large enough area at the back to throw away all of the waste. The vehicle itself was white, and the box on the back was painted Brunswick Green, with a Harry's logo and all the associated livery in a bright and distinctive yellow.

There was just one last thing to check.

The sketches I had been given in Australia allowed for a padlock to be fitted to the mower ramp, but they didn't specify any locks on the shelving units. As a consequence, I had made sure that I rented an apartment with a lockable garage, so that I could leave all of my equipment safely in the vehicle overnight. I had confirmed the van's dimensions several times and measured them against the width of the garage door beneath my apartment. According to my calculations, everything should fit, but there was only one way to be sure.

The first journey I undertook in my new vehicle was one of about ninety feet, where after a couple of broken U-turns, I managed to line up the van to my garage's open door and drive, more or less, straight in. With the vehicle's roof fitting safely under the door and the fender resting just short of the wall, I checked in both side mirrors to confirm that the tail was safely inside. Mission accomplished.

Or not, as it happened.

Working from a written set of specifications, I had checked the width of the vehicle against the garage interior, but failed to take account of the fact that I would of course be seated behind the wheel at the time - an oversight that became clearly apparent when I first opened the door, as it travelled all of about four inches before hitting the wall. It was a similar scenario on the passenger side, and as I sat in my brand-new, purpose-built van, it soon dawned on me that (given I hadn't exercised a sunroof option), I was effectively trapped.

I felt like a complete fool, but rather than bid an immediate and embarrassing retreat, I spent the next few minutes tuning the radio (just in case someone was watching) and the next couple of years loading equipment in and out of the garage at the start and end of each day.

Having eventually come to terms with the ramifications of my miscalculation, I called a new client who had seen one of my flyers.

Stephanie Beattie lived in a two-story house on Milbank Avenue - a stone's throw from my place.

She worked as a freelance journalist, did occasional voice-over work, and was studying for a degree in astrology. Her house was adorned with a massive, tangled wisteria that hovered over a front garden that consisted of two hugely overgrown shrubs, set amid a number of concrete pavers, that were loosely covered in tiny colored pebbles. It may have been a small garden, but the list of "things to do" was long, since Stephanie asked me to dig out the two shrubs, sweep up all the pebbles, lift up the pavers, lay some new turf, plant a couple of small hedges, prune the wisteria, and fit some chicken wire to her wrought iron railing fence.

None of the tasks particularly fazed me with the exception of tackling the wisteria. It certainly needed attention, as it was already wrapped around various telephone cables and disappearing beneath the gutters and roof. It looked as if it was trying to wrestle the building to the ground, but my client was more concerned with the fact the plant had failed to produce any flowers for the past few years. Mind you, she was somehow under the impression that she had an "expert" on the case, so apparently that was the least of her worries.

I started by sweeping up the pebbles and shoveling them into thick, plastic "rubble sacks," before lifting each paver, disturbing a hidden, subterranean world populated by crawling insects and bugs. I cut down the two shrubs, dug out the roots, and turned over the soil with a fork.

Thereafter, my first real foray in my Harry's vehicle was

to a local landscape supplier, where I had ordered a few yards of turf to lay in Stephanie's front garden. The turf itself was grown in New Jersey and had cost me $3.00 a square foot. Had I purchased the very same stock in the nearby retail garden centre, it would have cost me $7.50 a square foot. Quite a mark up, but it had of course travelled across the road by then.

Dealing with a wholesale landscape supplier made me feel quite privileged, given I was "in the trade" and consequently able to solicit much cheaper prices and plenty of advice.

I returned to Stephanie's house, laid the turf, and watered it in. I thought it looked terrific, and I was thrilled at the transformation I had created. Fortunately, so was she. Brimming with confidence, I vowed that tomorrow I would tackle the wisteria.

As luck would have it, one of my neighbors had given me a book titled *Pruning*, some weeks before. It had a couple of pages solely devoted to wisteria, with detailed instructions of how and when to prune, together with an illustration of a plant that looked nothing like the one I was confronted with. The plant in the book had a neat, uniform shape, with a handful of lateral vines shooting from a central trunk. By comparison, Stephanie's wisteria looked as if it should be on some sort of medication.

I studied the text meticulously, and the next day, I tackled the job with an extension ladder, a pair of secateurs and a sense of foreboding. I might have done just as well with a whip and a chair. *Pruning* outlined a method that was supposed to ensure great bunches of flowers would burst forth the following spring. But it was difficult, if not impossible, to follow this method when my first priority was simply to tame the beast. Thick, sinewy strands invaded every tiny crevice, clinging fiercely to cables and siblings alike. For the first hour or two, I ignored the textbook and simply hacked the vine into a vaguely manageable state, before trying to deploy some of its more subtle principles.

When I finished, Stephanie's wisteria bore little resemblance to its former incarnation. It was practically bald and neatly confined behind a series of wires that I had stretched across the front of the house. Its thicker branches were punctuated by short offshoots, all pruned back to the third bud.

Only time would tell whether or not the operation had been a success, and I must have studied that wisteria's progress dozens of times over the following months, aided by the fact I had to pass Stephanie's house on my way to the Chinese takeout. By early spring, I could see a few buds forming, and I watched intently as they swelled and grew. It wasn't long before the entire plant was draped in a mass of plump, gray pouches. They seemed to be hanging from every stem, until one day they all burst forth in a spectacular festival of color.

At that point, my business card featured a list of services printed at the bottom: garden maintenance, hedge trimming, rubbish removal, and the like. I was seriously thinking of adding wisterias as a specialty.

Chapter 24

Squirrels

Buoyed by my recent success, I made an appointment with Mrs. Phillips, who lived on Connecticut Avenue. She had picked up one of my flyers and called me at home the night before.

Mrs. Phillips had lived her entire life in the company of her mother, much of it in their current residence - a house named, appropriately enough, "Squirrels." Young Mrs. Phillips (as I referred to her) was sixty-five, while her mother, Nasty Mrs. Phillips (as she once referred to herself) was ninety-three. They became an intellectual sideline for me, as I spent no small amount of time over the next couple of years trying to decide which of the two was the more insane.

When I first pitched up at Squirrels, it was Young Mrs. Phillips who answered the door. She was short and plump with straight, gray hair that was cut and shaped into a bob, which sat above her shoulders. She wore thick spectacles that magnified her eyes to a frightening degree and spoke with a high-pitched shrill, fueled by generous amounts of saliva.

"Yes!" she shouted, staring at the embroidered logo on my shirt. "Harry's Landscaping! Yes! Hello!"

"Who is it, Susan?" came a quivering shout coming from the living room.

Holding the door open, Young Mrs. Phillips looked over her shoulder and screamed, "Gardener Mommy!"

"What?" Nasty Mrs. Phillips shouted in reply.

"Gardener Mommy!" Young Mrs. Phillips shouted back.

The exchange continued for some time, before Nasty Mrs. Phillips (protesting that she couldn't hear), waddled out of the living room. Propped on a walking stick, she stood next to her daughter.

Young Mrs. Phillips shouted in her mother's ear, "Gardener Mommy!"

Nasty Mrs. Phillips fixed me with an angry stare and pointed with her stick.

I hadn't even introduced myself before she let rip with a tirade of abuse. She had been let down in the past by gardeners who hadn't shown up, or who had quoted a job, only to present her with an invoice for an amount in excess of what had been agreed, trampled the flower beds, kicked the dog, scratched the car, and pretty much ruined her life.

I expressed my sympathy for the appalling treatment she had been subjected to in the past and assured her that I would do everything in my power to complete any job I undertook to her complete satisfaction. She didn't believe a word of it, and quite frankly neither did I, but at least we managed to move on and debate the cost of mowing the lawn.

Presenting a quote to Mrs. Phillips times two, was like trying to negotiate a mass redundancy with a couple of militant labor unionists. I suggested thirty dollars - a quote that was greeted with absolute derision. Given there was a tall pine tree growing in the middle of the back lawn, depositing no shortage of cones on the grass (all of which would have to be gathered up before the grass was cut), the job was probably worth at least forty. But I had to factor in the entertainment value of dealing with two of the neighborhood's more colorful characters, and we finally settled on twenty five.

I had managed to establish something of a rapport by this stage and agreed to do the job right then and there, when Nasty Mrs. Phillips put me firmly in my place. She stepped forward on to the porch, with the handle of her walking stick resting in the crook of her wrist. She put her right hand on my arm and raised her left, pointing at me with her index finger. Wagging it inches from my face, she chided me, "Now you listen to me, young man. You are a colorful Aussie, but a very naughty boy!"

I took what I needed from the vehicle - strimmer, mower, safety goggles, and especially, ear defenders, when Young Mrs. Phillips was kind enough to give me a crash course in lawn mowing. She even showed me how I could adjust my own equipment. Apparently, if I lowered the height of the deck on the mower, I could cut the grass a little bit shorter. Gosh! Thanks, Mrs. P.

I set about strimming the edges as precisely as I could and I carefully raked up every single pine cone before mowing the lawn with the neatest and straightest lines I could manage. I was about two thirds of the way through, just coming up the slope, when I could see Nasty Mrs. Phillips wobbling across the terrace. I mowed up to the top of the lawn (pretended I couldn't see her), then turned around and headed back down. I stopped at the bottom of the garden and emptied the contents of the catcher into a sack, hoping that that she might get bored, go back inside, and fall asleep. No such luck.

I slowly pushed the mower toward her, pausing at every opportunity, hoping that she might turn her back just long enough for me to execute a swift U-turn and run back down to the bottom. But there was nothing I could do. She had me cornered, and I simply couldn't ignore her any longer. I walked to the top of the slope and tried to act surprised when our eyes met.

"Hi, Mrs. Phillips," I said, smiling.

Nasty propped herself on her walking stick, her right hand shaking furiously, as she gestured toward the front of the house.

"Can't you do a better job with that front lawn?" she shouted, furiously. "It looks absolutely dreadful!"

She was clearly unhappy, but I was gravely offended. I mean, I may not be the most experienced, qualified, or even capable gardener, but I wasn't about to stand there and have the quality of my work questioned in such an ill-informed and aggressive manner.

I reached forward and switched the throttle off on the mower. I stepped toward her, looked her squarely in the eye, and said, "I haven't done it yet."

"Oh," she said.

CHAPTER 25

AN OFFER I COULDN'T REFUSE

I had been told that the journey from Greenwich to JFK would take around fifty minutes, so I allowed myself an hour and a half. Thankfully, on the day that Jason was due to arrive, the traffic wasn't too bad, and I figured any time I spent on the road was only generating exposure for the brand. Short of its actual delivery, this was effectively my Harry's vehicle's public launch. Painted bright green and yellow, it was impossible to miss, and I waved politely as other cars sped past, thinking that perhaps my first franchisee might be seated behind the wheel.

Jason's flight was on time, and after a couple of laps of the terminal, I saw him emerge from immigration and customs. He was dark, stocky, and understandably tired. It was by now mid-afternoon and I was anxious to get underway before the rush hour traffic started, so we made use of the mower box for Jason's suitcase and hit the road.

On the way back to Greenwich, we shared our history with Harry's. Jason's measured more than a decade, while mine, to date, had lasted a matter of months.

After leaving school, Jason had worked as a clerk for a customs agent and having long harbored an ambition to work for himself, seized the opportunity to become one of Harry's very first landscaping and lawn care franchisees. He made a great success of the business and later invested in a regional franchise that covered much of Melbourne's North West. After succeeding with that venture, he had helped to start the Harry's Trees division and had worked his way up through the ranks again, although he did point out "that was five years and about fifteen kilos ago."

Jason and Harry were quite close and occasional squash partners, which I found really encouraging. Together, they had seen the business become a large and diverse network - one that spanned the entire country, and I couldn't see any reason why we shouldn't be able to achieve something similar in the United States.

Once we arrived at my apartment, I put the tea kettle on and introduced Jason to the sofa bed, before ducking out to finish a couple of regular mowing jobs.

One of these jobs was for a young Swedish couple who lived well out of range of Young Mrs. Phillips and just around the corner from the ill-fated Lisa Pullen. Matthias's job had relocated him from Stockholm to New York. His wife, Ida, stayed at home to look after their baby daughter, Elvira, and the biggest dog I had ever seen.

When I arrived, Ida was standing outside the front door, cradling her sleeping child in her arms. All the while, she assured me that their Great Dane was "still only a puppy," as he stood up on his hind legs and rested his paws on my shoulders. Being quite tall myself, I often found it slightly unnerving to meet someone who was as lofty as me. Never before had I met a dog that was.

I wondered if the dog was perhaps a manifestation of Scandinavian pride, as Ida proudly proclaimed that Elvira was named after the title character in the famous film. Not wanting to broadcast my ignorance of Swedish cinema, I quickly fetched the mower from the vehicle and set about mowing the lawn. The grass was quite long and damp in patches, where the branches of a couple of fruit trees hung over it. Some of the apples that they dropped were huge, and though often rotten, they made useful missiles, as I booted a number of them into the garden beds.

I had to be careful strimming and mowing the Swenson's lawn, since I often found myself concentrating too much on neat edges and straight lines, rather than the low hanging tree branch I was about to collide with - episodes that were as infuriating as they were painful. All too often, I found myself rubbing my head and cursing. Needless to say, any apples that fell as a consequence, I didn't so much kick into the garden beds, as launch against the fence.

Returning to my apartment, I was pleased to see that Jason was still awake and had made himself at home. I left him busily typing an email, while I rustled up a Spaghetti Bolognese. Hopefully, Jason's body clock would allow him a decent night's sleep, since the next day we would be visiting some of my regular customers.

We started at Jo Breen's house, before we did a circuit of

regulars that included Mrs. Martin, Stella Cole, and Sally Ann Bolt. For the most part, Jason strimmed while I mowed, which provided me with an interesting insight as to how well and how quickly two people could work together from one vehicle.

The fact that Jason wielded the strimmer like a wand only made our efforts more productive. When I strimmed a client's edges, I was grateful not to kill anything, or at the very least not to scalp the lawn, whereas Jason raced around with the sort of precision that suggested he had been doing it most of his working life - which, to be fair, he had.

There may have been an embarrassing gap in our respective skill sets, but it was still a worthwhile exercise, as there were some simple tips Jason conveyed, which would help me to work a little more efficiently and that I could hopefully (one day) pass on to a franchisee.

We spent the rest of that week, and much of the next, working together, which gave Jason a modest insight into the American market and me a better understanding of the Harry's system and structure. During the day, we would mow lawns, do quotes, and shift the odd piano, while in the evening we would talk all things Harry's. Soon, however, it was time to do battle with the traffic and make a return trip to the airport.

A few days after he got back to Australia, Jason emailed me. He was still very much committed to developing the business in the US and suggested that perhaps we would be better off working together. Rather than him operating on a national basis, with me solely responsible for New England, he proposed that I relinquish the rights to New England and instead take a 30 percent stake in the entire US business. Thereafter, we would try to sell a 10 percent share to a group of investors, who, hopefully, would provide a sufficient amount of working capital for us to effectively launch Harry's throughout the entire US. He attached a copy of a prospectus that spelled everything out, and it all seemed to add up well to me.

I emailed him back and said, "Thanks very much for the offer. Let's do it."

CHAPTER 26

THE TRASH MONSTER

My new vehicle was already paying off. It was eye-catching, distinctive, and a very effective marketing tool. People were stopping to speak to me in the street, and it was certainly a lot more practical when it came to loading equipment on and off, to say nothing of the fact I could cart all the trash in the back. Above all, I felt proud to be behind the wheel, making me even more confident when it came to quoting jobs and dealing with the occasional awkward client.

The only downside was that as Harry's Landscaping and Lawn Care was a commercial enterprise, I wouldn't be able to use the local trash dumpsters any longer - at least not the residential ones. I had been travelling to them at least once a week for a couple of months, always managing to convince those in charge that the trash I was disposing of was indeed mine and from my own property. Clearly the fact that I was unfailingly dressed in a Harry's uniform wasn't enough to undermine that.

From now on though, I would be classed as commercial,

and required to dispose of my green waste in a hitherto hidden and uncharted world - a dark and sinister chasm, concealed behind the domestic façade of the Holly Hill Household Waste Disposal Site.

Entering this area was like stepping on to the set of a science fiction film. It covered about three acres and held massive piles of processed waste that was stacked thirty feet high. Mountains of muck had been crushed, mashed, and fast-tracked as compost and fertilizer. I drove slowly past each one as a thin vapor of deodorizer wafted from a series of jets that were mounted on the perimeter fence.

The entire area was patrolled by a single "Trash Monster." Dark, unshaven, surly, and ugly, he operated a front-end loader, scooping up great swathes of waste, shifting them about, and arranging them into different piles. He didn't speak, so much as grunt, and every day, he seemed determined to be even more rude and arrogant than the last. I think he probably lived there, making his home in one of the many compost mountains and existing on a diet of month-old fruit and rotting vegetables.

In the far corner of the plot, there was a single pile of raw green waste. I backed the van up, opened the rear doors, and lowered the tailgate, so that I could add the contents of my own cargo to the pile. I had done a couple of garden clean-ups during the week, so the vehicle was full of spiky brambles and branches, all tangled and tightly packed, having been repeatedly stomped upon by a middle-aged Australian in a pair of size 13 Blundstone boots.

To my surprise, the Trash Monster offered to help. He

had seen me struggling to extract so much as a twig from the back of the van, and rather than see me spend the rest of the day engaged in a kind of garden waste tug-of-war, he suggested that we run with his idea. It was a simple enough plan. He would drop the fork of his loader into the back of my vehicle. Once it was firmly wedged in place, I would drive a few feet forward, then all (or at least most) of the rubbish would end up on the ground.

Well it seemed like a good idea at the time.

At first, the monster didn't manage to get much of a purchase on the contents, so I reversed and we tried again. This time, we had a measure of success. I could feel a great weight lifting from the back of the van, as I drove forward. I stopped, got out, and was delighted to see that that we had managed to deposit about half the contents of the bin on the ground.

If only we had stopped there.

Unfortunately, we decided to try one more time. I sat in the driver's seat with the engine idling, while the monster maneuvered the loader into position. I wasn't sure exactly what means he used to control the movement of the fork, but could only assume that he didn't call upon his brain to any great degree.

All of a sudden, there was an almighty crash, and I was hurled around the cab, banging my head on its ceiling. I flung open the door and jumped out, just as the monster was reversing from the scene of the crime. He blamed the wind and the fact that I had driven off too soon - an ambitious claim, given my vehicle was in neutral with the parking brake on. In any case, he had managed to plunge the fork into the back of my (now no longer new) van. There were deep gouges in one of the rear doors, both sides of the bin were dented and splayed, to say nothing of the fact it was now impossible to close the tailgate. It was an ugly sight. To be fair, it was only a work vehicle and little more than a steel frame with painted aluminum panels, but I still wanted to cry.

I dragged the rest of the rubbish out by hand and surveyed the damage. The box was still more or less intact, though badly scratched and horribly misshapen.

The Trash Monster climbed down from his machine, shrugged his shoulders, and produced an acrylic strap, complete with hooks, buckles, and some kind of a bracket. He fixed a hook over the railing at the top of the box, stretched the strap across the other side, and started to winch the two together. At first, I didn't expect him to achieve anything, but I was pleased to see the box slowly return to something like its original shape - well, to a certain degree. Soon, I was able to shut the rear doors and close the tailgate (albeit with the use of my shoulder).

It was a strange feeling, thanking someone for carrying out a rudimentary repair to a vehicle he had so recently obliterated, but given there wasn't another dumpster site for miles and I had no other viable waste disposal options, I couldn't afford to start an argument.

I drove away from the dumpster site and tried to put the whole episode behind me, fearing all the while that it would in fact be the box that ended up behind me, since owing to the recent episode it might break free from the chassis and crash on to the road.

Luckily, that didn't happen, and I managed to arrive at Mr. and Mrs. Young's house with the vehicle intact. Given they lived within walking distance of my apartment they had received one of my flyers, and I had been mowing their lawns for the past couple of months.

Rather than leave my van outside on the street, I chose to drive in and park on the Young's pebbled driveway. I managed to open and shut all of the side doors and mower ramp, extract the necessary equipment, and complete the task, before starting the engine and heading off to the next job.

Rear visibility wasn't great in the vehicle, since I only had two side mirrors to work with, and I was definitely still angry about the recent incident at the dumpster site. At least those were the two excuses I gave myself, shortly after reversing into the Young's veranda and breaking the corner of a tile that sat between a brick and wooden post. The tile was more aesthetic than structural, but since it was just outside the front door, it was impossible to miss.

Given the last time I was there I had managed to demolish a terracotta plant pot (being a bit careless with the leaf blower), I could sense my reputation (such as it was) being seriously undermined.

Neither of the Youngs were at home, so I raced to the hardware store and bought a small bag of cement (not bothering to solicit any advice), and set about trying to repair the damage. I would, of course, confess to the crime, but I was anxious to do what I could to lessen its impact. Having absolutely no knowledge or experience of bricklaying to the extent that I didn't even realize I should have been mixing the cement with other materials such as sand, the exercise was a complete waste of time.

I left a note (the gist of which was "I'm afraid I've done it again.") and decided at that point to call it a day. I drove home, put the cement in the garage (where it stayed for the next few years), and sat around feeling rather sorry for myself. That evening, I bought an expensive bottle of wine, presented it to the Youngs, along with an apology, and an offer to mow their lawns a couple of times for free. They were both very reasonable about the whole thing and accepted quite graciously, before I walked home. After all, I dared not drive.

Chapter 27

Anatomy

The next day, the most extraordinary thing happened. Lisa Pullen rang.

I felt sure she must have dialed the wrong number. I mean, until I had arrived on the scene, she had been the proud owner of a perfectly healthy, colorful, and thriving rhododendron, yet bizarrely enough she did actually want to speak with me.

Lisa had decided to redesign and replant much of her garden. Even though she had hired a professional horticulturist to select an array of suitable plants, she wanted me to do much of the preparatory work. I was both surprised and delighted to be given the opportunity, and we made an appointment to discuss the project.

I arrived at Lisa's house the next day, and we strolled around the back garden, managing to avoid any mention of the "chainsaw incident." Her plan was to build up the existing garden beds with extra top soil and replant them, before dressing the lot with chunky pine bark chips. My job was to extend some of the beds, re-turf a few small sections of lawn, then cart in and rake over the soil and bark - something even I should be able to manage.

As we wandered past one section of the garden, Lisa explained how she intended to prune and shape a couple of shrubs and a small tree that was encroaching on the access to her children's play area. It was a simple enough job and one she had left out of my original brief.

"I can do that for you," I said enthusiastically.

Lisa leapt between me and the plants in question. "No, you won't!" she said, extending her arms, as she shielded me from her precious garden. "I know what you're like!"

I thought it was fair enough.

It wasn't long before I was back at the landscape suppliers, ordering two tons of topsoil and a huge pile of bark chips. Logistically, the job was going to prove a bit of a challenge, since gaining access to the garden in order to deliver the soil wouldn't be so easy. Lisa's property backed onto a quiet street, and my contact and I had concluded that it might be possible to lift the bags of soil and bark over the fence and lower them into the garden, using the crane fitted to one of their flatbed trucks. As long as we could pull up close to the curb, it shouldn't be a problem, and given the garden beds would themselves be empty, all we would need to worry about was clearing the fence.

Timing would be an issue, however.

Greenwich was very much a commuter town, with many of its residents and those of the surrounding towns making their way to its train station each weekday morning, to travel to New York. Strict parking restrictions applied close to the station, but Lisa's house was on the fringe of the free parking zone. But if the commuters got there ahead of us, we wouldn't be able to pull up next to the curb. As a result, the crane wouldn't be able to reach over the fence, which would leave us no option other than to leave the bags of soil and bark on the sidewalk. I would then have to wheelbarrow everything in through the back gate and up a set of steps, which needless to say, would be far from ideal.

We hatched a plan.

We would load the truck first thing in the morning and be "on site" by 6:30 a.m. I would meet the driver acting as a guide, while he operated the crane. The idea was to pull up next to the curb before the commuters' cars began arriving. But just to make sure, I gathered a number of traffic cones that I would set up in the street the night before. That way, I could cordon off an area large enough for the truck to pull in, just in case any cars arrived before we did.

It seemed as though we had all the bases covered. I drove up the night before and placed each of the cones in position. I set my alarm for 6:00 a.m. and was on site as the truck arrived. As it so happened, the driver did a good job of getting into the street at all, since it was already clogged with parked cars, including along the stretch that I had so carefully cordoned off. A number of drivers had clearly chosen to ignore my blockade, but one or two had been kind enough to collect each of the cones and stack them up next to a tree, so it wasn't a complete loss.

We were left with no other option than to lower each of

the bags on to the sidewalk, since the arm of the crane couldn't possibly reach over the fence from the middle of the road.

The driver operated the crane as I stood by.

"Mind the fence!" I said any number of times, "but scratch as many cars as you like!"

Our original plan had failed, but at least we had managed to deliver all of the materials. The issue now was how best to transport everything to the other side of the fence. Rather than shovel the soil into any number of wheelbarrow loads and negotiate a path through the back gate, I decided to simply launch it all over the fence a spade full at a time. The garden beds were clear, so I wasn't likely to destroy any plants, and as long as I didn't throw the soil across the lawn or bury a small child, I should be okay.

Once the soil was safely on the other side of the fence, I would spread it across the beds, before launching the bark chips in a similar fashion. I adopted a backhand stance, digging into the soil and hurling the contents over my right shoulder. A couple of excursions into the garden confirmed that the soil was landing safely and well within the confines of the bed itself, so I carried on.

The novelty of throwing soil over a seven-foot fence wore off rather quickly, and it was really quite depressing to see another huge bag of soil sitting right next to the one that I had barely made an impression in already. I decided that I would rake the soil out after every twenty or so throws, just to break the monotony. Eventually I emptied the first sack to a sufficient degree, that I could drag it inside and tip what remained on to the garden.

I now had one large bag on either side of the fence, and I raked what I had thrown smoothly and evenly before setting about the second sack. It was hard work, but eventually I managed to get all of the soil and all of the bark on the other side of the fence. The beds were nicely built up, and I was really pleased with how it all looked. I then watered the bark down with a hose.

That was when I first felt the pain in my wrist. I imagined the various muscles and tendons in my arms were cooling down by this stage, aided perhaps by the odd splash of water, but I was surprised that I hadn't detected any discomfort before now. The pain in my right wrist was such that I couldn't even hold the hose, let alone turn off the tap. What's more, it was only getting worse. I cradled my arm in the tail of my shirt, gathered all my tools, and the empty sacks, before making my way to the emergency room at the Greenwich Hospital.

I was of course already registered (courtesy of Mrs. Stigger's psychopathic canine) and grateful that someone was able to attend to me more or less straight away. I sat on an examination bench and explained to a nurse what I had been doing, and how quickly the pain had arisen. She carefully massaged and probed my hand and wrist. She didn't think any bones were broken, but as she prodded and probed the joint itself, we soon arrived at a conclusion.

"Tell me if this hurts?"

Her query was greeted with a resounding "Yes!" as I violently squirmed, writhed, and practically leapt off the bench.

The nurse immediately diagnosed tendonitis, and explained (with the aid of a wall chart) that hurling a large quantity of soil and bark chips over a seven-foot fence, was not something the human wrist was actually designed to do.

She prescribed rest and a course of anti-inflammatory tablets. I was okay with the second bit but couldn't see where I'd get the time to fit in the first. I was then fitted with a brace that bound an aluminum strip to my arm by means of three Velcro straps.

I didn't realize it at the time, but that brace and I would spend several months together.

Chapter 28

Meet the Neighbors

One of the great testaments to the marketing power of my vehicle was how many neighbors of my existing customers became clients themselves.

Such was the case on East Elm Street, where I had done a couple of mowing jobs for a woman who lived in a housing association property. My client's elderly neighbor had approached me just as I was loading my equipment.

"Know anyone who does lawn mowing?" she asked.

I was standing about two feet to the left of a massive Harry's Landscaping and Lawn Care logo and replied, "Well, oddly enough, me."

We walked back to her property, and she explained how she lived on the first level of a two-story corner house. A portion of the front garden was her responsibility to maintain, as was most of the back. Her name was Mrs. Marsh - Annie to her friends and Mad Annie to me.

From the outset, it was clear that she was quite a character. For someone so old and frail, she had tremendous energy, a wicked sense of humor, and a thoroughly stubborn demeanor. She asked me for a quote to mow her front and back lawns as "the neighbors had been nagging her about it." She was clearly living alone, and given I already had a client next door, I quoted her twenty dollars for a job that was, to my mind, worth thirty.

"Oh no," she said emphatically, shaking her head from side to side.

I thought her reaction was pretty harsh, but before I could justify the price with my usual preamble of strimming edges, collecting and disposing of clippings, full insurance cover and so on, she chirped back, "Forty."

"You're not supposed to haggle up," I said, but she insisted, explaining that she wanted to make sure I would do a good job and that I would keep coming back. I assured her that each time I did, I would find a few other jobs to do (of which there were many), so I could be sure she was getting value for money. She agreed and put the kettle on, as I went to fetch the mower.

I became a regular fixture at Mad Annie's and over time maintained her entire garden. She wasn't exactly shy when it came to airing the "family laundry," and there were certainly times when I could have done with a little less detail regarding her recent operations and visiting boyfriend. All the same, forty dollars in cash was always placed under a porcelain figurine in her lounge room, which I generally retrieved after a cup of coffee and a sandwich.

We spent a lot of time talking, and I was often reminded that she wasn't exactly fond of her neighbors. She ripped into "the one on welfare" next door, "the bloody cow upstairs,"' and "that evil witch" across the lane. By the same token, she was tremendously generous to me, and it was rare that I ever left her house without clutching a can of soda or a bottle of wine.

I soon learned how important "scheduling" was when it came to working for Mad Annie. She lived across the street from an elementary school, and to find a parking spot within a reasonable distance of her house when school let out in the afternoon was impossible. Being Greenwich, every weekday at 3:00 p.m., the road would be clogged with a fleet of late-model SUVs. It was as if an invasion force had descended upon the school gates, waiting to receive its final orders before the assault on Stamford.

One day, I had no choice other than to park several hundred yards away. I pushed the mower along the street and carried all of the tools that I was likely to need. I managed to finish the job (and my coffee) before the heavens opened, but once they did, it started raining heavily. I didn't particularly fancy getting a thorough soaking, so I gathered all of my equipment, left it on the corner of the street, and made a dash for the van. I drove back and parked on the corner of a narrow lane that bordered Mad Annie's property - admittedly in a no parking zone. I had lowered the ramp, lifted the mower inside, and opened the side shelving units, when I first met Annie's neighbor - the one who lived "across the lane."

She was a very angry, nasty, and aggressive woman, who was wearing a heavy, black raincoat and holding an umbrella. Suffice it to say, she was less than impressed that I had parked where I had. I tried to explain that my vehicle was originally parked about half a mile away and that I was simply trying to avoid getting drenched, but she was having none of it. She became quite hysterical and marched toward me, screaming something about "ignoring civic responsibilities." By this point, I was already soaked to the skin and responded that if I didn't have to spend so much time trying to explain myself to her, I probably would have finished and left by now. All of which didn't make the slightest impression, since she stood (safely dry) shouting at me from little more than a foot away, while pointing at a sign erected on the edge of the pavement.

I had by now given up trying to reason with her, when she stepped forward, almost taking my eye out with a spoke of her umbrella. She fixed me with a furious stare and spat "What if an ambulance had to get through there?"

By this stage, I had just managed to load my last piece of equipment onto the van. I slammed the door shut, turned toward her, and said, "Well, madam, if it was coming for you, I don't think anyone would care."

CHAPTER 29

THE BEST FORM OF DEFENCE

Oddly enough, the same school that was inadvertently the cause of that altercation in the first place became a client itself, or at least part of it did. The local council was supposed to maintain the grounds surrounding the preschool (which was part of the elementary school), but they had proven to be so unreliable and their service had been so poor, that I was contracted to the task.

It was a tricky job, because I had to negotiate a path in and around an array of climbing frames and playground equipment, while my performance was carefully monitored by an audience, that some weeks numbered in double figures.

I could never see or tell what activities the teachers had assigned to the male children in particular, but whatever it was, it clearly paled in comparison with the spectacle of a man with a lawn mower.

The first time I tackled the job with a class in session, I glanced over my shoulder to see someone looking at me from the window. It was a little boy with his hands raised above his head, his tiny face pressed against the glass. His face lit up when I raised my thumb to him, and sure enough, the next time I looked across, he had been joined by two others. On my next pass, three became five, and soon it was standing room only, as the entire window was lined with little spectators.

I was often grateful when clients were not at home. That way I could just get on with the job without the pressure of being supervised or timed, but this was a whole different ball game. By now, a dozen potential critics lined the circuit. Shielded by panes of glass, they looked like they were all housed in a corporate box, and I wish I could have done something more spectacular to amuse them. Even so, it seemed the combination of noise and motion was entertainment enough, since I managed to hold their attention for the entire duration of the job. I could have sold tickets.

Conscious of the time, I waved goodbye to the kids, loaded everything onto the van, and drove off, as I had an appointment with a fellow called John Smalls, a local realtor.

John's agency had been hired by the owners of a massive property to find a suitable tenant for a recently renovated office unit on their land. John had emailed me a brochure to me a few days before, and as far as I could see, the unit was well located, the right size for Jason and me, and no more expensive than a couple of others (in much less desirable locations) that I had considered as the national office for Harry's USA.

My commute had taken me through a delightful, winding country road, which made the drive very scenic and relaxing. Following a set of written instructions and a crude map, I drove into the estate, while admiring the magnificent mansion on top of the hill. The office complex was situated next to a lake, and though completely refurbished, it had retained its original layout, structure, and charm.

John was waiting for me when I arrived, and I am willing to bet he had never closed a deal as quickly as he did that day.

Unit 4 was a single-story office with four allocated parking spaces. It was rectangular in shape, with its original rustic wooden beams exposed. Furthermore, it had plenty of natural light and included a kitchen and bathroom. It was a unique facility in a wonderful location. I thought it was perfect, and pending Jason's approval upon his return to the US, we would take it.

The fact that I managed to enlist a new client while I was there was something of a bonus. Gladys Wood lived in a small cottage that adjoined Unit 4. She had worked as a housekeeper at the estate for most of her life and was rewarded in her retirement with a quaint and delightful residence, complete with a small, picturesque garden. She tended to the flower beds herself and grew a few vegetables in a greenhouse, but there were two or three medium-sized trees that were getting a little out of hand, so she asked me if I knew how to prune them. Of course, I said that I did (having made such a spectacular success of Stephanie Beattie's wisteria) and believing that I would find sufficient reference in *Pruning*, I agreed to return later that week to tackle the job.

I had bought a set of long-handled "loppers" from SiteOne, which had helped to make light work of jobs such as this in the past. But I fear, I got carried away with a little too much gusto. I cut off one branch, then another, which set something of a precedent, and before I knew it, I had pruned one entire side of a tree pretty much back to its trunk.

It looked a bit severe, but I had no choice other than to prune the other side in a similar fashion, since any other approach would be an admission of error. As I did, however, my heart began to sink. What had been a healthy and robust tree only minutes before now resembled a small totem pole. Worse still, Gladys had just opened the back door and was now walking toward me in order to make an initial inspection.

At first, I panicked but then decided that the best form of defense was attack.

"Mrs. Wood!"' I called out enthusiastically (greeting her like a long-lost friend). "I'm really pleased you're here. Let me show you what I've done."

I explained how concerned I was that the tree I was pruning was located quite close to the clothesline and that in its former guise, it really was quite dangerous. After all, it only took a second to lose an eye. In any case, I had pruned it back quite heavily (apparently) to stimulate a new and more robust growth spurt, and what looked quite harsh now, would in fact pay off down the track with a rich and full foliage.

I had almost managed to convince myself at this point and stood there nervously waiting for her to respond.

Gladys (God bless her) looked at the "tree" and nodded her head, saying, "Yes, okay. Well I can see you know what you are doing."

CHAPTER 30

THE GREENWICH TSUNAMI

I'd always been fascinated by the diversity of accents in the United States. If you were to travel across the country, you would find people speaking quite differently. Some accents were quite easy on the ear, while others not so much.

For example, I quite liked a lot southern accents - at least, I quite liked Alison Kirkbright's southern accent. Alison lived in Pemberwick, but she was originally from Georgia. She was friendly, attractive, and the mother of three children. Alison became a semi-regular client, which meant I was called upon to mow the lawns, when her own children had either refused or made a mess of it, and also to trim a conifer hedge that divided her front garden from a neighbor's driveway. Chatting with her was like going away for the weekend. She was always friendly, and I often entertained myself (while working) by mimicking some of her phrases and expressions.

When I first met her, she drove a burgundy-colored minivan - a vehicle that was perhaps a little bit of Georgia transplanted in Connecticut. Regrettably, that vehicle didn't last, and it was replaced by a silver SUV, something more befitting the Greenwich stereotype. Pity.

Paula Wilks, by comparison, drove a navy blue Renault Espace the entire time that I knew her. Respect. She was originally from North Carolina and lived on Dearfield Lane.

One of the very first people to have received a Harry's flyer, she was actually at home when I had delivered it, and she'd confessed to making sure the door was locked when she saw me coming down the drive. Luckily, she found the time to access the website and was encouraged by the fact that there was a substantial organization behind the huge circus animal making its way up the street.

Every "Harry" should have a client like Paula Wilks. I referred to her property as the "Dearfield Tea Rooms," given every time I arrived there to do anything, she would produce cups of coffee, freshly baked muffins, cakes, cookies, and bars of chocolate - even if I was working next door. I mowed Paula's lawns every two weeks. I put up fences and a trellis, landscaped the back corner of her garden, planted a few trees, and generally did whatever tasks sprang to mind. How I didn't put on weight remains a mystery.

One day, I pulled a few weeds from her children's vegetable garden and was presented with a "check" from her four-year-old son. It was a series of doodles with a figure vaguely resembling a two scribbled on a Post-it note. I thought it was a very generous payment for less than a minute's work, and to this day, I haven't had the heart to deposit it.

Carina Gustavsson completed my local triumvirate of clients. She was beautiful, Swedish, and lived around the corner on Grove Lane. If Carina didn't win the Greenwich best dressed title year after year, she was a cinch to finish in the top ten. Whether she was hitting the golf course, going out to lunch, or just hanging around the house, she always looked immaculate, which presented an interesting contrast with my grass-stained uniform and muddy boots.

I tended to her lawns every couple of weeks and was called upon to do pretty much all there was to do outside. I trimmed the hedges, dismantled an old green house, pressure washed the paving, deck, and outdoor furniture.

One day, she asked me to clean the roof of the carport. The roof itself was little more than a number of clear plastic sheets attached to a wooden frame, and as it was essentially flat and sitting directly underneath a large pine tree, it was sagging beneath a weight of pine needles, twigs, water, and moss.

Carina accepted my quote to clear it all away, and I returned early the next day to find that frost and ice had been added to the equation overnight. I had no intention of getting up on the roof itself, since one slip would surely see me crashing through and onto the roof of an almost new Land Rover. Instead, I set a ladder against one side of the car port and fixed a wide broom head to an extension pole. That way I didn't have to actually get up on the roof, yet I could still reach across its entire width to gather all of the mess.

It seemed like the perfect plan.

I climbed up the ladder to a height where my waist was

just below the level of the roof and launched the pole across. As luck would have it, the width of the broom sat perfectly within the confines of each plastic sheet, so I was able to gather most of the muck and at the same time, contain it within a single, narrow channel. I drew the pole toward me, pulling as hard as I could, not realizing a number of things. Firstly, there was more water, ice, and muck collected there than I had first thought. Secondly, it was freezing cold, and third, I had no realistic means of escape.

I was perched several rungs up (at what I considered to be ankle-breaking height should I decide to jump), watching a gathering tsunami of ice, moss, and pine needles rolling toward me. It was like wading into the waves at a surf beach in midwinter, as a filthy, icy torrent flooded my shorts. My body froze and my heart raced, as I let rip with a breathless scream. It felt like I was being stabbed by hundreds of tiny ice daggers, while the filthy surge ran down my legs and into my boots. I fiercely clung to the ladder, shaking and shivering, all the while cursing the abominable winter climate.

I managed to climb down, and fearing hypothermia might set in at any second, ripped off my boots, wrung out my socks, and ran barefoot back to the van. It was a five-minute drive back to my apartment, where after a shower and a change of clothes, I returned to the fray- this time exercising a more careful and measured approach.

Chapter 31

The Little House

The next day, I drove to Nicola Gill's new place. She had recently moved from her house in Riverside to "The Little House" on Maher Avenue. Either the bloke who built the place was called "Little," or it was someone's idea of a joke, because no reasonable person could possibly describe any aspect of her new property in such modest terms.

The house itself was anything but little, and the surrounding property, which included an orchard, was huge. It had a large lawn at the front and an even bigger one alongside. There was a patch of grass surrounded by a conifer hedge (I reckon it was once a tennis court), some steep banks that would have to be strimmed, and grass just about as far as the eye could see.

I had always refused the opportunity to invest in a riding mower, as I didn't have a realistic means of transporting one. By the same token, tackling "The Little House" with my twenty-one inch Honda would be a full time job in and of itself, since by the time I would finish strimming and mowing, I dare say that the grass I had first cut would have already grown back.

I suggested to Nicola that I could get her a good deal on a riding mower at SiteOne. She agreed, and the following week, I was back in the saddle of her brand-new John Deere. I scheduled the job for every other Friday afternoon. That way, I could stagger home exhausted but have the weekend to recover. The whole job took about four and a half hours to complete, and I was often impressed and grateful that Nicola went to such lengths and travelled such distances, just to bring me a cup of coffee.

Her two sons returning home from school added an additional health and safety dimension to the exercise, as Toby (in particular) enjoyed following me around on his bicycle, and I certainly didn't fancy explaining any sort of a collision to his mother.

One day, Toby and his younger brother, Lucas, were running around, just as I was clearing the last few clippings and leaves from the driveway. Toby was standing close by, when I cheekily blasted him in the face with a shot from the blower. He laughed, thought it was a great prank, and asked me to do it again. I thought it was a bit rude to leave his brother out of the loop, so I gave Lucas a turn as well.

Suffice it to say, he felt rather differently.

At first, he didn't react at all, and it looked to me as though he was collecting his thoughts before embarking on a course of action. Then his bottom lip started to quiver, and I could see tears welling up in his eyes. At this point, I could see I was in trouble, and I suggested that perhaps Toby might like to step in and do what he could to comfort his brother and remedy the situation. Being older (I think he was about seven), Toby wasn't the least bit concerned and he assured me that his little brother was "always doing that." I looked back to see Lucas was now in full crying mode, and worse still, he was heading over to the house - to the sanctuary and comfort of his mother's arms.

I felt sure I was just minutes away from being sacked, and I pleaded with Toby to intervene, but he just hopped on his bike and rode away.

I weighed the options and decided that trying to explain and apologize to Nicola (and Lucas) didn't really appeal, so I loaded up the van and left.

If anything was to come of it, I would just tell her his brother did it.

Chapter 32

The Ultimate Upper Body Workout

The entrance to Stoney Ridge Lane looked just like any other on the Greenwich landscape, tucked away as it was, just beyond the roundabout at Riverside. Yet the road itself was once a very grand driveway that led to a magnificent stately home. No remnants of the old mansion remained, but judging by the size of the oak trees that lined the street it must have been quite something in its day.

Once the original house had been demolished, the grounds were redeveloped as a residential estate. Dozens of two-story houses were built on large blocks, all in the same style and all bordered by beech hedges. Curiously, every single property on Stoney Ridge Lane had a name. God forbid that its residents would have to tolerate anything so common as numbers.

Mr. Dorban lived at "Hill Stone." He had been referred by a friend and needed someone to trim the hedge at the front of his property, since "the fellow who normally does it has hurt his shoulder." Apparently it was "that time of year again" when the hedges had to be trimmed, and Mr. Dorban suggested that if I did a good job, his friend and neighbor across the street would be interested in having his done as well.

I hadn't tackled a beech hedge before, and I wasn't too sure just how far back it should be cut, so I set about it slowly and carefully. As it happened, Mr. Dorban turned out to be a pretty good coach. At one point, he took hold of the hedge trimmer and ran a couple of swipes for me, expertly angling the blades to achieve a neater, smoother finish than I had been able to achieve up to that point.

It took me three goes at it, but eventually the hedge passed inspection and a couple of days later, I was giving the hedges at "Cawdries" a similar treatment across the road. By the time I completed that job, I had been asked to quote two others.

I had plenty of other work booked and was having trouble getting out of Stoney Ridge Lane at all, as each job I secured seemed to lead to another. I dealt with Mrs. McIntyre at "Bend Oak" and spent an entire day working for Stewart McLaren at "Sandmount West," before Mr. Todd from "The Robyns" asked me to trim all of his hedges - front, back, and sides.

Having seen and trimmed enough hedges to last a lifetime, my interest and enthusiasm were fading, and I am the first to admit that I didn't do a particularly good job at "The Robyns" - at least not the first time around. I finished the hedges and shoved an invoice through the door. Later that night, Mr. Todd called me. He wasn't happy with the job I had done and asked me to come back and do it properly before he would pay me. I was tired, angry, and thought my arms were about to fall off, but I returned early the next day, insisting there couldn't possibly be anything wrong with it.

Mr. Todd had the advantage of being able to survey the site from an upstairs window, so I set my ladder up to replicate his view as best I could. I managed to perch myself both high and far enough away to see over the top and I had to admit he was right. The hedges I had trimmed looked like a scale model of the Andes. They were indeed bumpy and uneven, to say nothing of the fact that several twigs and shoots were sticking up indiscriminately. I gave each one another pass with the hedge trimmer, and once satisfied they were straight and even, I left a note and packed everything into the van.

Just as I was about to leave I was collared by a neighbor - a South African IT consultant who worked from home. He lived at "Absolute Wanker" - at least that's what it said in my work scheduler.

Needless to say, his property was surrounded by beech hedges. I took an instant dislike to him and added an "aggravation fee" to my quote, which he had the temerity to accept. I carried on with the job right then and there, which he personally supervised throughout, as he pointed out minor errors and oversights, insisting they be corrected immediately.

He wandered in and out of the house a few times, and at one point, he returned drinking coffee and eating a handful of cookies - neither of which he offered to me. It was the closest I ever came to walking away from a job.

Still, Stoney Ridge Lane was proving to be the ultimate upper body workout. After wielding a gasoline driven, hedge trimmer attachment for hours on end, to say nothing of raking mountains of clippings and hurling them into the back of the van, it was little wonder that I had the shoulders of an East German breast stroker.

My last beech hedge trim was for Mrs. Forster who lived at "Glenwood," right on the bend of the road. From the front of her property, I could see the entrance to Stoney Ridge Lane itself. It was like seeing a light at the end of the tunnel.

Her front hedge wasn't too big or too bad, and I managed to get it trimmed and tidied in about an hour. The property was quite long and narrow however, with beech and conifer hedges running the entire length of the backyard on both sides.

I worked my way down the left, negotiating a path through the flower beds, raking out as many of the clippings as I could, when Mrs. Forster wandered outside and handed a check to me. She thanked me for doing such a good job and explained that because she had to take her daughter to a dancing class, she wouldn't be back until much later in the day. I thanked her very much, wished her all the best, and started eyeing off the trampoline that was sitting in the middle of the lawn.

I had worked on several properties that housed trampolines before and had never considered having a go at it myself, but for some reason, I was inextricably drawn to this one. Aside from the fact my client wasn't at home and would not be coming back for some time, I think perhaps the lure was a desire to celebrate the end of the Stoney Ridge Lane hedge-trimming season.

Once I had finished the hedges on the other side, raked up the clippings, and blown the last few shreds next door, I loaded everything on to the van and returned to the back garden. Mrs. Forster's car was no longer in the driveway, there were no lights on in the house, and I doubted any of the neighbors could see, much less care, so I whipped off my boots and jumped aboard.

My first few forays were nervous and clumsy, but I soon found my timing, and it wasn't long before I was happily bouncing to a decent height.

It was time to turn a few tricks.

Given I was breaking a twenty-year trampoline drought, I wasn't overly confident that I could pull off even the most basic maneuver and decided to provide myself with some boisterous commentary, as a means of motivation. According to my delusional fantasy, I was one simple execution away from victory in the world championships and convinced that millions were watching, glued to television sets around the globe.

I bounced up and down a few times, building the tension to a fever pitch before stretching my legs in front of me, landing on my backside, and bouncing up again. I managed to straighten my legs on the descent, just enough to stay upright and maintain enough elevation to continue.

The crowd went absolutely mad, and the title was mine.

I raised both arms in the air, declared myself aloud to be "an absolute bloody champion," and then caught sight of two young girls standing just outside the back door of the house. They were both carrying small backpacks and dressed in school uniforms. I dare say it was Mrs. Forster's elder daughter and a friend. They looked like matching bookends, as they stood side by side, with their jaws dropped and mouths wide open.

It took me at least three or four bounds before I came to a halt. I climbed down, pulled on my boots, and proceeded to inspect the frame of the trampoline, confirming that the platform was indeed secure and level. I tapped the edge of the mat firmly, said aloud, "Yeah, that'll hold all right!" and walked out.

Chapter 33

Moving On

Winter had well and truly set in by the time Jason was due to return to the US. The days were getting shorter, but the Connecticut landscape was rendered all the more spectacular as a consequence. Exploring some of the narrow, tree-lined lanes that surrounded Greenwich was a joy, and when the sun did shine, it took the edge of the cold.

The next day I did battle with the roads and traffic, as I drove to the airport to pick up Jason. He intended to stay in the US for about six weeks before flying home for Christmas and returning in January. I certainly didn't envy him the air miles.

A couple of days later, I introduced Jason to Bob Lawrence, who had prepared and filed all the necessary documentation to enable Harry's Landscaping and Lawn Care to incorporate in the US. We hadn't managed to enlist as many shareholder investments as we had originally hoped, but more importantly, we had a company, a presence, and a plan.

I was particularly anxious for Jason to see our possible new office and described it in quite glowing terms to both he and Bob, assuring them that it was "a hundred times better and yet no more expensive than some dinky little office above a shop on Greenwich Avenue." I could have perhaps chosen a more appropriate comparison, given we were sitting in Bob's dinky little office above a shop on Greenwich Avenue at the time, but fortunately he didn't appear to take any offense.

Jason agreed that the office was in an ideal location, and we offered to sign a three-year lease.

We modeled the Harry's US website on the Australian version, and subscribed to a couple of franchise "matchmaking sites." Jason's experience in compiling all of the concepts in our information pack was already proving invaluable, to say nothing of his experience in recruiting franchisees.

Our first serious inquiry was from a fellow called Tim Gosden. He was working as a production manager for a packaging firm and was in search of a complete lifestyle change. As luck would have it, he lived in Stamford, which wasn't all that far away from me in Greenwich, and I was impressed (even a little intimidated) that he seemed to know every bit as much about the Harry's franchise opportunity, system, and structure as I did.

Tim had certainly done his research, and the prospect of coming on board with us as our very first franchisee seemed to excite him to no end. We spoke at length on the phone, and I think he did a better job of extolling the virtues of a

Harry's franchise than I could have. I only wish I had taken a few notes.

We arranged a meeting with Jason at my apartment, and I was pleased that Tim wasn't put off by the domestic environment. In fact, I think if we had presented him with a contract right then and there, he probably would have signed it. Instead we followed procedure and arranged for him to spend a couple of days "in the field" so that he could get a genuine insight into the business.

I really enjoyed working with Tim. He was very enthusiastic, hardworking, and lots of fun. There was probably more that he could teach me than I could him (from a practical perspective anyway) but I was sure that he found it a worthwhile exercise, even if Nasty Mrs. Phillips did berate us for conducting a "Mothers' Meeting" on her back lawn.

I introduced Tim to my van and assured him that it was in fact almost new, despite its rather battered appearance. He seemed quite impressed by its concept and design, and I explained that even though the business in Australia had been built on the back of thousands of trailers, I was convinced that vans were a more realistic option in the US.

Tim took a copy of the franchise agreement with him, giving every indication that he would sign it, as Jason and I were busily making preparations to attend another franchise exhibition in Boston. The exhibition was effectively the same show that I had attended the year before, and I hoped that this incarnation would prove to be more productive and enjoyable.

We had secured a small corner booth, with a couple of

banners that we had adapted from Australia and a few pieces of equipment that we had managed to borrow from SiteOne. It wasn't the most spectacular display at the event, but it was far from the worst. We stood there for the best part of two days, meeting and greeting people, while handing out brochures and business cards.

It was interesting to see the vast range of franchise opportunities on display. A number of lawn treatment companies were exhibiting, as were various cleaners and printers, but I didn't see any franchise that was comparable to Harry's.

We did our best to enlist some interest and collected about fifty names and addresses of people who had asked for more information. As it so happened, the most promising inquiry came to us on the next day, from a fellow who had seen my van in the parking lot, but he hadn't been able to locate our booth. I thought if we did decide to exhibit at the event again, we could just park outside and save ourselves a small fortune.

Returning to Greenwich, I tended to my regular clients while Jason did the rounds of the local realtors. He was looking to rent a house that would accommodate his wife and family, as they would be coming over from Australia later in the year. Within a couple of weeks, he managed to find a house in Glenville, which was a fifteen-minute drive north of Greenwich and about the same distance to the new office.

Jason's move to Glenville more or less coincided with us taking possession of the office, and since Tim Gosden had kept in touch, it was exciting to see things starting to take shape. We even had an additional parking lot constructed for us by our office landlord, who was concerned that my van might "cheapen the setting," should it be parked within the confines of the office complex itself.

We had the phone and Internet connected, while we installed desks, computers, printers, and a meeting table. Adding a large Harry's Landscaping and Lawn Care logo to the door completed the baptism, at which point we locked everything up and took a road trip to New Jersey.

Harry had hired a call center to handle the bulk of our franchise inquiries and job leads, and they had sent us what seemed like a genuine inquiry from an address in Trenton. I was looking forward to the trip, since it was an opportunity to meet our new colleagues, and we thought the Trenton inquiry sounded quite promising, given the people we had arranged to meet already operated a successful landscaping business.

It was very disappointing to drive for several hours, only to find that the Trenton address didn't exist, no one was now answering the phone number we had been given, and the whole inquiry had been clearly nothing more than a hoax. To add insult to injury, someone tapped on the window of my vehicle and asked me to give him a quote to trim his hedge. I said that I would love to help, but since I didn't have a single piece of equipment on board and had just driven from Greenwich, it probably wasn't the best time.

Chapter 34

Marketing

I was gradually building a base of regular clients but chose to continue supplementing my income by working weekends at a couple of farmers markets in Hartford. On Saturdays, I sold all types of tomatoes that had been grown in poly tunnels and greenhouses in New Hampshire, and on Sundays, I barbecued lamb burgers for an eccentric sheep farmer from Massachusetts.

The Saturday market was set up in a parking lot, just behind a row of shops on the main street. Every morning, a couple of farm employees would load dozens of tomato-laden plastic crates onto vans, before dropping individual batches off at various market locations in and around New York and Connecticut. I aimed to arrive before 9:00 a.m., which gave me enough time to assemble an interlocking metal stand that was packed in a heavy vinyl sack and left sitting under a tree with all of the day's stock. It was like playing with an elaborate erector set, and it generally took me a couple of goes at it to master its assembly. Once it was intact and standing, I laid four plywood boards over the top of the frame, and they in turn were covered with a couple of rolls of artificial grass.

As a rule, I built a mountain of beefsteaks to my right. Next to them was a tangled pile of cocktail vines, then several punnets of cherries and santas, bordered by heirloom vines and various tubs, bottles, and jars containing all manner of tomato-based sauces and toppings. It was quite a colorful display, and I took no small measure of pride in its presentation, even if my sales technique and general attitude was a little more irreverent.

For the most part, the market was populated by genuine farmers, many of whom had travelled from as far away as Vermont. By comparison, I was a complete fraud but the politically correct stance (stipulated by the market management) was to purvey the myth that I worked all week on the farm and that I had woken up very early to pack all of the stock before hitting the road. Under no circumstances had I driven from my apartment in Greenwich.

Customers often asked me, "How are things in New Hampshire?" Some recalled childhood holidays and their own trips to the state. Having never set foot in the place, it was a challenging bluff to maintain, and as much as I managed to pull it off most weeks, I did think it was best to come clean once or twice, when I was really pressed.

The tomatoes themselves were delicious and consequently very popular. Most weeks, the time simply flew by, as I busily emptied punnets and vines into paper bags and restocked the display.

It was a social outing as much as a weekend job and I made a lot of friends with customers and stallholders alike. Foremost among them was an eight-year-old tom boy called Lottie. She came to the market most weeks, when she wasn't playing soccer for her little league team and would wave furiously from the front seat of the car while her mother searched for a parking spot. She wasn't the least bit shy and had as much charm, character, and assertiveness as anyone I had ever met.

When I first met her, I told her that I was an Australian and asked if she knew where that country was. She most certainly did, then I knelt down to her height and added, "I'm from Melbourne."

She wasn't the least bit impressed and looked quite nonplussed. "Never heard of it," she said.

A succession of eastern Europeans looked after both the bread stall to my left and a large, pretentious organic fruit and vegetable operation set up on my right. Occasionally, the market manager squeezed a goat cheese vendor between us. "Goat Man" presented his goods dressed like a lab technician, and when I made the mistake of remarking that I didn't realize the process of making his cheese was such a science, he swiftly corrected me.

"Actually, it's more of an art," he said indignantly.

I didn't bother speaking to him again.

Pearce set up opposite me most weeks, selling Buffalo meat, mozzarella cheese, and yogurt. He was what a lot of American people would describe as a jerk. He had waist length hair tied back in a ponytail, wore shorts year-round, supported the Boston Celtics with a passion, and could talk underwater with a mouth full of marbles. People thought he was either a great character (as I did - for the most part anyway), or an absolute pain in the neck. A rather dry-witted customer of mine summed him up (for many) one day, when he said that Pearce was living proof of the widely held theory that "under every ponytail is a horse's ass."

I really enjoyed working with the tomatoes, since most of my customers were very pleasant and friendly. It was rare that anyone suffered my zero tolerance policy when it came to rudeness or complaints about prices.

I remember chatting to a fellow one day who asked me what I did for work when I wasn't selling tomatoes. I was too busy to try and explain the whole Harry's franchise thing, so I opted to tell him of my secondary vocation and said that I was writing a novel. He nodded approvingly and returned a few minutes later when the rush had died down a bit.

"I have thought of a publisher who would be interested in your book," he said.

"Really?" I said excitedly, thinking that I might soon launch myself from weekend tomato vendor into the realms of the literary elite.

"Yes!" he said. "The Lord Jesus Christ."

Suffice it to say, I was a little disappointed and asked him what might be the amount of any advance I was likely to negotiate with his "publisher."

"The best advance you could ever hope for!" he said. "Forgiveness for all your sins."

I said, "Thanks very much, but if it's all the same to Him, I would just as soon have the cash."

I worked on Saturdays for a couple of years, and because of the seasonal nature of the produce, I managed to have the winters off. The market was like a cashless economy, since each week I left with an armful of vegetables, bread, and cheese, all bartered for by exchanging any excess stock of tomatoes.

My Sunday job was in Bristol, a suburb of Hartford. My employer was a woman called Mary. She lived and worked alone, was grossly overweight, and a larger-than-life character. Mary drove a battered old Subaru, which towed a small livestock trailer. Each week it was weighed down with a heavy gas powered barbecue, a dozen or so coolers full of meat, three or four plastic tables, a couple of umbrellas, and assorted junk.

The market itself was set up in a courtyard opposite a small park and at the end of a narrow lane that housed a number of small antique shops. Twenty odd stalls were packed into a small space, and at peak times, it was very crowded. I was banished to the fringes, which made sense, given the smoke and fumes the barbecue generated. All the same, it worked quite well, since I was able to service the passing trade as much as the market's own customers, even if I was exposed to the elements.

I drove myself to the market most weeks but scored a lift from Mary early one Sunday morning. She had lost her power overnight, and as a result, she hadn't been able to grind any of the shoulder joints that she used for the burgers.

It was a minor crisis, so she asked if we could execute the process at my apartment before we made our way to the market.

It was just before 8:00 a.m. when I could be seen carrying several clear plastic bags stuffed with raw meat into the building that housed my apartment. A generous trail of blood ran along the footpath and regrettably, all over the carpet and stairs in the hallway. I had already incurred the wrath of my neighbors after traipsing mud and grass clippings through the entryway, but this was something else entirely. With each step I took, I dreaded being accosted by Barbara - my erstwhile nemesis in apartment number one. She was the godmother of the "building's Mafia" and had made a point of asking me to "please" preserve its new carpet only a few weeks before.

Mary and I must have looked like a couple of serial killers who were desperately trying to dispose of a body, and even though we managed to escape unnoticed and unscathed, I half expected the local police to break down the door any second. Suffice it to say, I think the entire episode was a damning indictment of the Greenwich neighborhood watch program.

Once we had arrived at the market, unloaded, and set the barbecue on its feet, I scooped up fistfuls of ground meat and shaped them into neat patties before grilling them. I cut the hamburger buns in half, placing them in baskets, while Mary laid out an array of sauces and condiments. The market opened at 10:00 a.m. and most days, we were busy from the outset and absolutely crazed by lunchtime. Within an hour or two, Mary usually managed to sell out everything except for a few sausages. But by then, she was able to shape more burgers and slice more buns to help fuel the lamb burger juggernaut.

People waited in long lines as we were often running at a hectic pace, acting very indifferently to those who inquired if the meat was organic. Mary and I often complimented each other on the thinly-veiled barbs we gave in response.

I heard one terribly proper woman ask Mary one day, "How are your joints?"

"Mine all ache," she said.

There was a great sense of community among the market's vendors. That may have been down to the fact that each week we were huddled quite close together, but I reckon it had more to do with the fact that the Camden Head Tavern was right next door. Many of us met there each week after the market closed, while one or two vendors would indulge themselves a little earlier.

Each week, Les could be seen nursing a pint of Guinness in his stall (just as soon as the pub opened) while he worked his way through a crossword puzzle, in between sales of chicken and duck.

"Hey, burger boy!" he called out one day. "Slang for Aussie farmer? Five letters."

The lamb burgers were good fun. The market had a friendly and relaxed vibe, and I could eat all I wanted for free. I had made some good friends, but it was hard work and I would get home quite late. After my obligatory Sunday night Chinese takeout, I would often fall asleep on the couch and start the working week feeling tired.

Sadly, it was time to leave the markets and focus on the bigger picture.

Chapter 35

Well, It Seemed Like a Good Idea at the Time

I came to regret putting an ad in the *Greenwich Sentinel*. Not so much because it was expensive (which it was), but because I lived more or less on the boundaries of its distribution and a lot of the leads it generated were too far-flung to even contemplate.

One worthwhile lead that I did secure, however, was in the neighborhood of Cos Cob, which was about ten minutes away. Julie Clarke lived on quite a busy road and one that housed the offices of a number of local businesses. She and her husband wanted to give their front and back gardens a thorough makeover, as they planned to put their house on the market in the spring.

They asked for the front garden beds to be cleaned out, turned over, and dressed with bark chips. They also wanted to put down a membrane that would stop the weeds from coming back and for someone to pressure wash the driveway and patio. There was more to do in the back. A row of dead conifers had to be cut down and dug out, piles of trash removed, and a whole section of lawn dug out and re-turfed. I wandered around the garden, making notes, drawing diagrams, and taking measurements, as snow began to fall. By the time I finished, it was snowing quite heavily and I explained to Julie that I would have to leave and source some materials, before I could give her a quote in the next couple of days.

It was snowing when I returned two days later and had barely let up in the interim. I knocked on the door, said hello, and gave her my quote. She thought it was "a bit high," and said she would have to speak with her husband before making a decision. I told her I thought that was perfectly reasonable. She then alerted me to the fact that none of the other gardeners she had contacted had yet bothered to show up, let alone provide her with a quote. I seized the opportunity and offered to get started on the job right then and there.

"But it's snowing," she said.

"That's okay," I replied, suggesting that I could get most of the hackwork done that day, and I'd return the next with the turf, bark, and a pressure washer.

She seemed impressed with my enthusiasm and told me to go ahead. I thought I had come up with the perfect solution to get the job, and I was actually looking forward to working in the snow. I gathered a few tools from the van and started digging out the weeds in the front garden as a thick white blanket gathered around me.

The novelty wore off after about five minutes. By then, my gloves and boots were sopping wet, I could barely feel my fingers, and I certainly wasn't having any fun. To make matters worse, it was now snowing even more heavily than before. I resorted to working in relatively short bursts, ducking under the front veranda every few minutes, ripping off my gloves, and furiously rubbing my hands together. I hated having to put them back on, but figured cold is fleeting, while blisters last. Even so, I was determined not to be defeated by the weather and kept working at a furious pace.

I weeded the front beds as if my life depended on it, cut down the dead conifer shrubs, dug out the stumps, and threw all of the trash in the back of the van. After rewarding myself with a burger deluxe for lunch, I returned to the fray, skimming the top off what lawn there was with a shovel, and turning over the ground with a fork. I then carefully raked over the soil and called it a day, just as it was getting dark.

It didn't appear to have snowed much overnight, but it was still bitterly cold the next morning. I called my landscape supplier and dumped a bag of bark chips in the back of van, along with several yards of turf, and made my way over to Cos Cob.

I thought it best to work from back to front. I would lay the turf on the back lawn and then spread the bark chips on the front garden. That way I could finish and clean up with the pressure washer. It was a simple enough plan, but I hadn't counted on the fact that the soil I had forked and raked the previous day would be frozen solid. Rather than finding an even surface of lush topsoil, I was confronted with a mass of frozen, gray clumps, which looked like a bunch of icy golf balls sitting in a bunker. I couldn't possibly lay the turf over them, and to make matters worse, what little sun there was would be shielded from that section of the lawn, owing to a shadow cast by the house. Consequently, it was unlikely to thaw for some time, and I made a start with the bark out the front in the hope that it would.

An hour later, little had changed, so I resorted to raking all the icy balls to one side and thereafter digging down a few inches below the surface. I shoveled the unfrozen soil into a wheelbarrow, raked the frozen clumps into the hole that I had just created, and top dressed it with the soil from the barrow. It was tedious, time-consuming, and potentially ineffective, but as far as I was concerned, it was working. I rolled out and pressed down each roll of turf, neatly trimming the edges and desperately hoping it would not subside during the spring thaw.

I then drove to Greenwich, where I had an appointment with one of my regular mowing clients. Miranda lived on the corner of what was a very narrow street. I had been able to park in her driveway in the past, but as she would be "coming and going," I would have to leave the van outside. That was all well and good until a couple of her neighbors felt the need to blast their car horns, alerting anyone nearby to the fact that they had trouble driving past, so I thought it was best to park on the grassy shoulder just outside her property.

Miranda had asked me to cut down a number of

branches from a large tree that was hanging over the house and prune all of the shrubs and hedges surrounding the lawn. Garden cleanup jobs like this would invariably accumulate two or three times the amount of waste and cuttings that I initially expected, and this one was certainly no exception. It was as if every branch, leaf, and frond had multiplied threefold once it hit the ground. In any case, I raked them all up, piled everything into the back of the van, and after jumping up and down on it all a few times, it was off to the dumpster.

Or not, as it happened.

One of the features of my Volkswagen vehicle was its front-wheel drive, which is all well and good if you are driving around on an asphalt surface, but a bit of a disaster if all four wheels are parked on a patch of damp grass with a heavy load of garden waste shoved in the back.

I started the motor, put it into first gear, lifted the clutch, and spun the front wheels. I then tried again with the same outcome. On my third attempt, I planted the proverbial "pedal to the metal" and went precisely nowhere. I was clearly in a bit of a bind and trying to think laterally, I decided that I would go in reverse and swing the van (albeit blindly) out onto the road. Nothing. With the weight of all the cuttings and waste in the back, lifting the front wheels ever so slightly off the ground, and no grip or drive at all emanating from the rear, the tires just spun and spun.

I jumped out and assessed the situation. After several attempts, I reckon I had managed to move the van about four inches - all of it downward, since both front tires had churned up the grass, gouging two deep troughs in Miranda's front lawn.

It was an ugly sight and a depressing situation. I resorted to dragging all the trash out of the back and piling it on the lawn, thinking that without the weight in there I might be able to extricate myself. I even tried wedging a couple of branches under the front tires, but short of digging up half the lawn, I had run out of options.

I called Volkswagen's roadside assistance and was assured that someone would come by and help me as soon as possible. I was able to occupy myself in the meantime by once again putting all of the waste in the back of the van. I also took the time to calculate the amount of topsoil and turf I would need to buy in order to repair the damage that I'd done. It went without saying that I would need to come up with a logical explanation as to what I was doing sitting in my vehicle, parked on a client's lawn for hours at a time, if any one asked.

It was pitch-black, 8:00 p.m., and over four hours later when roadside assistance finally arrived and towed my vehicle off the lawn. Even in the dim light of a streetlamp, the damage was obvious. I forked over the two deep depressions I had created and returned the next morning with a sack of topsoil, a meter of turf and a box of chocolates for Miranda.

Chapter 36

Prospects

Jason arrived back in the US, and I brought him up to speed with some of the franchise inquiries we had received in his absence. Oddly enough, one of those same prospects called me on my cell phone as we were driving back from the airport. It was a fellow called Trevor Morrison who lived in Massachusetts.

"I've just seen one of your vehicles on the expressway," he said.

Though he had effectively spotted the entire fleet, I didn't dare correct him.

"Really?" I said. "Could be anyone I suppose."

Trevor had found our listing on a franchise matchmaking website. He had read through the information we had sent him and was keen to know more. I made an appointment for Jason and me to meet with him later that week.

In the meantime two other prospects had surfaced. One was an accountant from Virginia, and the other a Coca-Cola sales representative who lived in Ohio. Both were quite capable gardeners in their own right, but they contrasted in almost every other respect. The accountant was in his fifties, had a professional background, and was married with two children, whereas the sales rep was single, twenty-five, and looked like he should still be in school.

Soon after, Jason and I arranged to meet Trevor at his house in Springfield. Trevor was in his early forties, was powerfully built, and looked like he could handle himself - something I made a mental note of, lest I spend too much time looking at his girlfriend. I let Jason do all of the talking, since he was vastly more experienced than I was when it came to explaining the Harry's franchise structure. I felt a bit like a third wheel, as Trevor alerted us to the fact his current job involved testing commercial aircraft for signs of metal fatigue. Jason explained the virtues and features of the Harry's system in great detail, but to be fair, I think Trevor was pretty much sold on the concept before we had arrived.

Something that struck me while we were there was just how much Trevor was looking forward to doing a job for someone that had the simple courtesy to say thank you when he had finished. I was able to assure him that I was thanked several times a day and often presented with cups of coffee, sandwiches, cakes and cookies, which seemed disproportionately generous in comparison with someone who helped to keep a commercial airliner up in the air.

Chapter 37

The Clapboard Ridge Mole Invasion

Jason's family entourage arrived in the US toward the end of February. It consisted of his wife, twin two-year-old boys, and parents-in-law. The plan was that they would all stay in the Glenville house with the in-laws heading home after a few weeks.

Jason was born in the US, but as far as I could recall, his wife had never even visited the country. In any case, it probably wasn't the best time of year to arrive - first impressions and all that. I imagine it was warm and sunny in Melbourne when they left, and it was anything but when they touched down at JFK. It was the middle of winter after all and consequently cold, wet, and dark. In hindsight, Glenville probably wasn't the best choice Jason could have made. It was a very pretty and expensive village but very quiet and populated by a lot of older people, who were perhaps less inclined to welcome a new member into their midst.

When I first investigated the local property options, I quickly dismissed the surrounding neighborhoods as too insular, and Glenville, for all its quaintness and charm, would have probably topped the list in that respect. I had never met Jason's family before, and to be fair, I barely knew him, but I regretted not suggesting Greenwich or Riverside as an alternative. In any case, renting a large family home in what was arguably one of the most expensive regions in the US was going to make a nice mess of the company's finances.

Sadly, it was clear from the outset that Jason's family relocation wasn't going to work out. Having the in-laws on hand kept a lid on the problem for a time, but things started to go downhill pretty quickly once they returned to Australia.

That issue aside however, the business was progressing. Tim Gosden and Trevor Morrison had both committed to spending a week in Australia, to attend the franchisee training course at the Harry's Group head office, while Jason would present the same course himself for Jody Church (the kid from Coca-Cola) at the office in Greenwich.

Wherever possible, we encouraged anyone intending to come on board to train in Australia. We could, and in time would, replicate the training course in the US but we thought that travelling to Melbourne would enable prospective franchisees to see for themselves just how vast and diverse the business had become.

I was by now combining the operation of my own franchise with working in the office, and I spent several days showing our prospects the ropes out in the field. One of my regular clients at the time was a couple who were both doctors and lived on a large property on Clapboard Ridge Road. The job usually entailed a lot of lawn mowing, and I was called upon to complete a few landscaping jobs and general garden cleanups every so often as well.

With the onset of spring, I noticed that a couple of small mounds of soil had started to appear in the lawn. Two soon became four or five, and a few weeks later, we were well and truly into double figures. The culprit was a mole - not a creature I was familiar with, but after some Internet research, I discovered it was a small rodent that was effectively blind and burrowed its way beneath the surface, devouring worms and grubs, while it constructed a network of tunnels in the hope of attracting a mate. Apparently, moles were quite common, and I was assured that the best way to get rid of them was by setting a trap.

I spoke with my contacts at the local garden center and bought a device that I could best describe as being like a very large clothespin. It was a stainless steel contraption, and the idea was to set it in the ground beneath one of the mounds. The idea was that the mole would then burrow through it, trip the spring, and be clamped around the neck, until someone (that is to say me) arrived, dug it up, and managed to repatriate the animal to a more suitable environment - which was a polite way of saying smash it on the head with a shovel.

The trap was a very simple concept and possessed a very basic construction. It was clearly conceived on the premise that moles were not only blind but apparently stupid, so I happily parted with twelve dollars, having been given every assurance that they in fact were.

I returned to the battleground and surveyed the site, trying to ascertain where best to set the trap. As far as I could see, a network of tunnels had been constructed in an entirely random fashion. Thinking the culprit was more likely to travel along one of its newer avenues, I dug under one of the fresh mounds while feeling around for the direction of the tunnel. I wasn't wearing gloves at the time, and I made as much noise as I could in order to frighten the beast away, lest it mistook my finger for a giant earthworm.

I set the trap and optimistically returned the next day to inspect it. Nothing had happened. The trap was still set, and there were no new mounds in the lawn. I vowed to come by and inspect it as often as I could. Three days later, there was still no change. But after a week, I found a fresh mound of soil less than a foot from the one where I had set the trap in the first place. It was as if the mole had constructed a bypass, specifically to avoid my clumsy contraption.

Determined not to be outsmarted by a small, blind rodent, I dug up the trap and set it again in the fresh mound, while filling in the tunnel beneath the original. My subsequent inspections only revealed more mounds and no moles. I was losing the battle and embarked on a simple war of attrition. Rather than invest in more traps or, for that matter, keep moving the original one about, I would simply leave the trap in place and afford the animal the opportunity to do the decent thing. It was either that or the mole's tunnel network would eventually reach capacity and then it would simply be a matter of time before mole and trap would coincide. Regrettably, I never got the chance, since my "mole role" was superseded. I found myself the victim of a modern day industrial revolution, when I was replaced by a high tech device, marketed by some charlatan masquerading as a wildlife specialist.

Apparently his device could be set up in the garden, where it would emit an uncomfortable electronic frequency, a sound that your average mole would find thoroughly ear piercing. The creature would then abandon its tunnel network and probably move next door, generating the prospect of another sale.

Personally, I favored patience and a shovel.

Chapter 38

Off the Mark

By the time the Clapboard Ridge Road Mole had won a clear points victory, our first two franchisees had returned from Australia, and given Tim had earned the right, he would be the first to sign his contract. Jason, Tim, and I convened at the office one evening, where we conducted a ritual that took just over two hours. Tim was tasked with selecting a zip code that would define his territory, as well as various other codes that would comprise his local and all areas.

Thereafter, we conducted a sign up interview and questionnaire, which seemed designed to root out anyone who might have fallen asleep during the training course. In truth, Tim had to demonstrate that he understood the contract and the extent of his obligations. We then arranged to supply his uniforms, advertising, and stationery. Equipment would be sourced from SiteOne, and his van had already been ordered from a local Volkswagen dealer. Jason signed the contract under a power of attorney for Harry, which I witnessed. Moments later, we had a check and our very first franchisee in the US.

Tim proved to be a great asset from the beginning. His launch meant we soon had a second vehicle on the road, and one that was being driven by someone who was enthusiastic, hardworking, and capable.

The accountant came on board a couple of weeks later in Virginia, followed by Jody Church in Pennsylvania, and Trevor Morrison in Massachusetts.

Tim in particular was a great help to me. We worked together on a number of jobs and notwithstanding the fact that at times I could barely keep up with him, we forged a worthwhile and enjoyable partnership. Fencing was a particular skill that Tim possessed and one that I was able to benefit from. It enabled us to add another service to each of our respective businesses. In addition to him being able to count on me as a reliable laborer, I could boast that he was a skilled craftsman.

Putting up fences together was good fun and earned us quite a bit of money, even though it was at times a trifle dangerous. Tim was quite a character, and many times, he would be holding a post in place while I was wielding a hammer.

"Okay." he would say. "When I nod my head, you hit it."

One day, we found ourselves installing a number of trellis panels for Paula Wilks, when her next door neighbor asked us if we could move a fence that bordered the rear of his property. Apparently, it had been encroaching on someone else's land since being reconstructed following a storm in

1987. It was a good thing we happened to be working next door that day; otherwise he might have had to wait another eighteen years.

Chapter 39

A Winter Exodus

Winters were difficult to cope with at the best of times. It was often bitterly cold, and losing daylight around five o'clock certainly took some getting used to. Working in the snow was by now off the agenda altogether, and even a quick stroll to the shops on Greenwich Avenue had to be carefully planned and executed. Snow that fell overnight would often thaw hours later, only to form a thin layer of ice on the sidewalk the following day. I was convinced this was why penguins had evolved to take such small, waddling steps, since executing a lengthy stride on a flat, icy surface could well result in a clumsy back-flip and a concussion.

It didn't come as a great surprise when Jason's family bailed out of the US and flew home. They had only stuck at the whole overseas adventure for a few months but had clearly been homesick and very unhappy from the outset. An unwelcome distraction at the best of times, it was a shame that it should coincide with the launch of our first few franchises. Jason would stay on for the time being and fly home in a month or so. Thereafter, he planned to commute back and forth between Australia and the US, staying in each country for about six weeks at a time. I didn't think for a moment it could possibly work, to say nothing of the fact we would be incurring significant travel costs and that the house our company was still renting in Glenville would sit vacant for much of the time.

There was little if anything I could do. I was a minority shareholder in a fledgling business and still finding my way when it came to marketing and managing a national franchise network. I wasn't drawing a salary from the company, and I had an expensive apartment in Greenwich to maintain, so I simply had to keep mowing and gardening during the day and come into the office on evenings and weekends, particularly when Jason was away.

Fortunately, we had a call center taking the bulk of our phone calls for job leads and franchise inquiries, while Jason and I put together information packets to send out to those who had expressed an interest. We had no shortage of prospects on the books, but of course it cost nothing to inquire. It was frustrating to work through a list of names, only to find that ours was often one of about thirty such information packets that some people had requested. It took a lot of time, sorting those with genuine potential from the time wasters, and it was very tempting to ask for the information to be returned, when it clearly had no chance of being acted upon.

The handful of franchisees that were already operating had made solid starts, and over time, I came to realize that the recruitment process was very much a numbers game. Of every hundred people that inquired, we would probably meet face-to-face with no more than five and could expect to sign one. We were effectively discouraged by numbers four and five because they simply weren't a good fit - although most of those people had come to the conclusion that Harry's wasn't the right opportunity for them anyway. But numbers two and three were particularly disappointing. They were invariably intelligent and capable individuals, who possessed all the qualities we were looking for. But more often than not, they simply didn't have the courage to make the leap from secure full-time employment to operating their own business.

CHAPTER 40

OVERLOADED

I was too busy working to drive Jason to the airport, and when he next flew back to Australia, I was meeting with Philip Walker and his wife in Greenwich. Mr. Walker had worked with one of the major banks for several years and had accepted an early retirement package, which enabled him and his wife to spend much of their time in Florida. He was a keen gardener and wanted me to look after their lawns while they were away.

The Walkers had decided to embark on a rather grand plan of their own. Their front garden was planted on quite a steep slope, and it was populated with huge, dark green conifer trees that often cast a shadow over the house. The trees dominated the landscape, and there was no room (and no point) in trying to grow anything underneath them. Their plan was to cut them all down, grind out the stumps, and start afresh with an entirely new array of colorful plants and shrubs.

I was flattered the Walkers would even consider me to do

the job, and I immediately referred the tree work to a local firm I had developed a relationship with. Down to Earth was located on a property outside of Stamford, and they had all of the expertise, equipment, and personnel to make short work of the task at hand. Once they had cleared the site, I would have a blank canvas to work with, and given I had yet to gather any real knowledge of plants, I commissioned my friend Sarah from the local garden center to help. She was a qualified horticulturist, who had helped me out several times before with some useful advice and the odd crash course in gardening over the telephone.

I explained everything to the Walkers, and they seemed perfectly happy with the arrangement. Down to Earth would clear the site, and Sarah would design the garden, while I planted everything out and installed a watering system.

Sarah and I inspected the garden together on her day off. Once it was all cleared, the area looked twice the size, but my friend clearly had everything under control. She had ascertained the acidity of the soil and considered the angle of the slope, measuring it against the shape and estimated height that the plants would eventually grow to. Her plan would ensure the garden was never devoid of color, as any shrubs that were dormant in the colder months would be compensated by others that bloomed at that time of year. She had certainly sold the concept to me, and the Walkers seemed equally impressed, asking us to go ahead. Sarah ordered all of the plants, while I would prepare the ground by digging in a great load of compost - and I knew just where to get it.

I had been dumping all of my green waste at the local dumpster site for twenty dollars a load, and this was my first opportunity to come full circle and buy some of it back. I left all of my equipment in the garage with the exception of a shovel, a rake, and a wheelbarrow, and drove into the trade section of the local Household Waste Facility. Mountains of steaming compost were piled just inside the trade entrance, and I went in search of the Trash Monster. He was sitting behind the wheel of his front-end loader "reading" a magazine. The compost was normally thirty dollars a ton, but apparently for today I could have two tons for the price of one.

I followed the monster back to the furthest pile and parked the van as he instructed. He then scooped up a great pile of compost in his bucket and dumped it in the back of my vehicle. I could see the body sink under its weight and thought for a moment that I might be better off taking it away as two separate loads. But before I could act upon my instincts, he had dumped another load in the back, and I was parting with my cash.

The monster gave me a receipt, and I climbed into the van as he left. Just sitting there, I could feel a tremendous weight behind me. I started the engine, vowed to take it slowly, and drove off. I reckon I had travelled about three feet before realizing there was a problem. The van could barely move, and I had to rev the engine mercilessly just to generate the slightest bit of movement. With the motor fairly screaming beneath my feet, I managed to build up enough velocity to actually register something on the dashboard. I had to, since there was a speed bump just ahead. Given the circumstances, it might just as well have been The Matterhorn. I thought I had no better than a fifty-fifty chance to get over it and tried to convince myself that if I could, it would be all downhill from there. Just how the gentle slope of a small lump of concrete was supposed to propel me another five miles, I really can't say, but I did manage to get over the bump and out through the gate.

By this point, I had gathered a degree of momentum, although there was a terrible burning smell. I thought it must be the weight of the box rubbing against the rear tires. Later I would discover that it was not in fact the tires that were burning to a crisp but the clutch.

I negotiated no less than three more speed bumps and made my way (albeit desperately slowly) out of the main entrance, but the modest gradient of the road leading up to the highway proved to be too much. I revved the engine as hard as I could and literally pushed against the steering wheel, but the burning sensation was now such that I felt sure something was about to explode, so I pulled into a lane that ran behind a row of houses, stopped the engine, and got out. The lane itself was covered with grass, and it clearly didn't see much traffic, which was just as well, because I certainly wasn't going anywhere for the time being.

My only option was to offload the compost, or at least enough of it, so that I could actually drive the van. The lane I had pulled into was very narrow, and there was no way I could possibly turn around. Since it led to a dead end, I would have to shovel most of the compost out of the back of the van, over the top of the cab, and on to the ground, otherwise I wouldn't be able to back up.

As it so happened, the nursery where Sarah worked was about half a mile away, and I was able to borrow a couple of large sacks that I might be able to sling the compost into. I didn't dare ask the Trash Monster for any help, since I couldn't imagine he would be allowed to take his loader off site, and given where I had parked the van, he wouldn't have been able to access it anyway.

I set the sacks out in front of the van, climbed into the back, and tossed the compost over the top of the cab, one shovelful at a time. Most of it landed where I was aiming, but by the same token, I think it was fair to say there was no better fed grassy lane in the country.

After about an hour, I had emptied two thirds of the load and felt brave enough to try again. I left two huge sacks full of compost sitting in the middle of the lane and backed out. Thankfully, the clutch held together, and I gingerly made my way to the Walker's, who, as fate would have it, had a property with a particularly steep driveway. I stopped outside and allowed everything to cool off - the engine, clutch, tires, and me, before making the final ascent. I eventually made it to the top of the drive, opened the rear doors, and went into shovel mode again. This time into a wheelbarrow, which I pushed across the lawn, tipping its contents onto the recently cleared slope at the front of the house.

Once I had cleared the entire load, I crudely raked it over the garden bed and returned to the lane. Backing into it, I shoveled the contents of one of the bags into the back of the van, drove to the Walker's, and repeated the exercise - twice. With all the compost now finally in place, I raked it over and forked it all in, mixing it thoroughly with the soil.

All of the plants were delivered the following week, and Sarah was kind enough to number each one corresponding to the diagram on her plan, which was wise, because names were entirely wasted on me. I stood all of the plants up in the back of the van, drove to the Walker's, and placed each one in position. It was nice to see the garden starting to take shape, and since most of the plants were already quite large, it wasn't difficult to see how everything might look in another year or two.

Once I had planted each one, I turned my attention to installing a watering system, which comprised about fifty yards of black plastic tube, fitted with various drip points and junction brackets. The idea was to connect a garden hose to the tube, which would then snake around the base of each plant. Each tube would be pierced and fitted with numerous drip points and plugged at its end, so that water could be dispersed evenly throughout the whole garden.

I cut the tube into three lengths, plugged each end, and connected them to a T-shaped bracket. I then lay the tubes across the garden bed, twisting each one around the base of the plants until such time as I was satisfied that they were all accommodated. It was a difficult exercise, but eventually, everything was in place. I connected the hose, switched on the tap, and stood back to admire my work.

Soon, the water started to drip and run down the slope.

I inspected the length of each tube, just to make sure there was sufficient pressure to ensure all of the plants would get a decent soaking. I was surprised to see water dripping quite freely from some sections but not from others. I climbed up, and assuming that water pressure was the problem, I turned the tap on further. The effect of which was that water freely streamed from the same sections as before, but not at all from the others. By now, most of the soil was so wet that it was impractical to climb down the slope to inspect the system, so I switched off the tap and explained to the Walkers that I would need to address a small water pressure problem the following day, when the soil had dried out.

I went home and sketched a crude plan of the system. The water was reaching the top of the slope okay, and there were no kinks in the hose at all. The whole layout was aided by gravity, yet some sections that effectively ran up the hill were working, while some of the lower portions were not. I simply couldn't understand it.

I didn't manage to solve the mystery until the following day. I walked around the garden, lifting each length of tube, and tracing it back to the original bracket the hose was connected to. At first, I thought the problem must be the bracket itself. But eventually I realized that what I had in fact done was connect both ends of the same tube to the one bracket, which, in short, meant that it was feeding back onto itself and that I had installed an entire length of plastic tube, littered with numerous drip points, that in actual fact, wasn't connected to anything.

I made the necessary and embarrassingly simple

adjustments, switched on the tap and then proudly informed Mr. and Mrs. Walker that I had managed to overcome the water pressure problem.

Chapter 41

Paving the Way

I had by now become great friends with a number of my clients. None more so than Stephanie Beattie, who was gradually giving her property a thorough outdoor makeover. Stephanie was kind, generous, and grateful for anything I was able to do for her.

She progressed with each individual aspect of the project when her finances allowed. She had erected a new fence, a pergola, turfed the back lawn, and replanted the garden beds, when she asked if I could help her by laying a section of paving at the bottom of her garden. Paving wasn't exactly my strong suit, but I had seen and heard about some of the tremendous landscaping jobs that Jody Church had completed recently and asked him to help.

Jody was developing his own franchise and building a base of clients, but it was still early days so I was able to convince him to come to Greenwich with the promise of a daily fee, a couple of takeout meals, and the opportunity to sleep on my sofa bed.

In the meantime, Stephanie and I paid a visit to my landscape suppliers, where she selected a range of Indian sandstone pavers and a couple of oak beams that would define the border of her lawn. We arranged for delivery to coincide with Jody's arrival, and I freed up a couple of days in my schedule.

Jody stayed overnight at my apartment, and we arrived on site the next day. It wasn't long before all of the materials were delivered and we had equipped ourselves with everything we were likely to need.

Stephanie's property backed on to a narrow lane that was quite difficult to access, so we had forty odd sandstone pavers and a large bag of hard core shingle lifted from the delivery truck and left around the corner. The sandstone was housed in makeshift wooden crates, which we had to break apart before we could cart each paver into position, while the only way to transport the shingle was a wheelbarrow load at a time.

Jody set about clearing and leveling the ground, while I carried each paver, leaning them against the fence. Once we had the site smooth and level, we barrowed in all the shingle, raked it over, and pummeled it into the ground with what the supplier shop called a "whacker plate." It was a flat bed of stainless steel, connected to a gasoline motor and set of handlebars. Once we started it up, the steel plate vibrated like mad, bouncing up and down, as it squashed all the shingle and soil flat and level. It was an exercise that otherwise might have taken us the best part of a day and one that was completed in less than ten minutes.

Jody started sorting through the pavers, leaving me to blend a mix of cement and ballast in the wheelbarrow. It was quite exciting to see him set the first paver in place, as I had never even conceived of undertaking a job like this before. He smeared the base of a paver with the mortar that I had mixed and pressed it firmly against the hard core base, using a spirit level to confirm its integrity. A second paver was laid, then a third and a fourth. Soon, we had created one complete edge and were working our way across to the other side. The project was certainly taking shape and it looked tremendous. By the time we had used up two barrow loads of mortar, about three quarters of the job had been completed, but it was getting dark and Jody was anxious to get back home, so he left me to finish everything off the next day.

After a quick refresher course in cement ratios, we tidied everything up and went our separate ways.

I returned the next day and confirmed that each paver we had laid was indeed level and set firmly in place. I then mixed the cement and ballast in the barrow just as I had done the previous day. I smeared the same amount on the base of each paver and on the scalping, just as we had done the previous day and followed the same procedure in confirming that each one was level. It all looked fine to me, so I left it all to set and meticulously cleaned and cleared everything away.

The next morning Stephanie called to say that she thought the paving and beams looked fabulous, but that some of the pavers were loose and wobbly.

No prizes for guessing which ones.

My site visit confirmed that all the pavers Jody had laid were set like stone, while all of mine were not. I could stand perfectly still on all of his and make the finals of a dance contest on most of mine.

I lifted each loose paver to find the mortar had stuck to the base. For the most part, it was set against the ballast okay, but for some reason, it just wasn't holding together. All I could think was that I had gotten the mix wrong, possibly adding too much (or too little) water. In any case, I lifted each one and started again. I mixed the mortar in the barrow, smeared the paver bases again, and made sure each one was level.

Once again, it all looked fine when I had finished, and once again when I checked the next day they were all loose, wobbly, and easily lifted. Clearly, cement and I just didn't get along, and the last thing I wanted was for Stephanie to suffer a fall, so I called Jody and asked him to once again drive over from Pennsylvania and fix it all for me.

That sofa bed was proving to be a good investment.

Jason was soon in Australia again, and I was working my way through all of our franchise inquiries as best I could. Already our modest network ranged in age from mid twenties to mid fifties, and there was certainly no "typical" franchisee, as we were clearly attracting people from a diverse range of backgrounds. Training was proving to be an issue, however. Some of our franchisees brought a useful array of skills and experience with them, but the important aspect for us was that they had a solid and clear understanding of just how the whole Harry's business was structured and how it all worked. Our preference had been for anyone planning to join us to travel to Australia beforehand, but that simply wasn't practical for many of them, even if we did fully cover the cost.

By this point, two of our very first franchisees had taken the opportunity to secure regional franchise rights. Trevor took on a sector that comprised much of Massachusetts, while the accountant secured the rights to Virginia. It was encouraging that two people had sufficient faith in the brand and the business to make such a substantial investment after only operating for about six months, but by the same token, we were still very much hamstrung by Jason's situation. He was spending as much time in Australia as he was in the US, which was proving to be very expensive, and I was finding it difficult to keep everything on track, while finding the time to operate my own franchise and simply pay the rent.

Chapter 42

Restructuring

We battled on for several months, while Jason did all he could to find someone who might be interested in buying his share of the business. His position was made all the more difficult by the fact that he had essentially "sold" the opportunity to a number of shareholders in Australia, and I can't imagine any of them would have been all that thrilled to know what was happening.

Harry's Landscaping and Lawn Care was still very much in its infancy, and given it was located and operating in the US, it wasn't a particularly attractive option for an Australian-based investor. Similarly, there were really only a handful of people in the country who knew just how successful the Harry's model was anywhere else in the world.

The business was suffering and growth had stalled. Jason was flying back and forth to Australia every six weeks, and he was clearly distracted while he was in the US. Over time, however, our Virginian regional franchisor expressed an interest in securing Jason's share of the business, and I did my best to broker a deal between them. He wasn't prepared to buy Jason out altogether, so the three of us settled on a deal, whereby he would secure an initial stake from Jason and thereafter retain the option to purchase the balance of his shares from future earnings. It meant that he now held a controlling interest and that eventually he and I would own the entire business. I thought it was a reasonable outcome, and everyone seemed happy with the arrangement. We signed the relevant documents, and Jason flew back to Australia. Logistically, it would prove awkward, however, as my new business partner was based hundreds of miles away in Virginia, but at the time, it was the best we could do and the only option we had.

I had by now started to scale back the operation of my own franchise, since I was spending a lot more time in the office before we employed a full-time administrator. Cathy Smith was one of several candidates that a local recruitment company had put forward. She lived nearby, was very experienced and capable, and over time, she developed an excellent relationship with all of our franchisees.

One of her first tasks was to organize an event, where we could present the new ownership structure to our existing network, along with our plans and goals for the future. We settled on a paintball venue in New Haven because it was more or less a halfway point from where we all lived and it featured an area where we could convene for lunch and make a short presentation, before we set about shooting one another. The day was a great success and the first part of our plan to firm up some important relationships. The second objective that we were anxious to complete, was for Harry himself to be happy and comfortable with the restructured US operation.

As luck would have it, Harry's Group was staging an Australian national conference in a few weeks' time, and we decided that I should attend. I caught a plane to Melbourne and soon after flew to the Gold Coast. I checked into the venue and wandered downstairs just as the four-day event was due to start. I stopped by the registration desk and said hello to Greg O'Brien, who said he was delighted to see me, since Harry was ill and had returned to Melbourne; therefore, I would be replacing him on stage to open the event.

Afterward, I spotted Jason, who confirmed that in a last-minute change to the schedule, he and I would be hoisted on stage in front of some five hundred delegates and armed with a microphone. Since at the time, he was holding several pages of carefully handwritten notes, I think it was fair to say he had been given a little more notice than me. Still, I quite enjoyed the experience. Jason and I sat together on stage, while Greg stood behind a podium "interviewing" us both. It was quite good fun, and given the fact I had just flown in from the other side of the world, I did rather enjoy my newfound celebrity.

I took part in all of the social activities and workshops, meeting people from various divisions and from all over Australia and New Zealand. On the first night, we were treated to a cruise on the river, while on the second, we attended a dinner in the hotel that was hosted by local impresario Dickie Dazzler, who was decked out in a shiny silver suit and wearing a bad wig. The event had a music theme, a trivia quiz, and God forbid a dancing competition.

Everyone seated on the six tables at the front of the room was given a number. I was number five. Over time, numbers one and three were asked to show off their dancing prowess, while the twos and fours were called upon for karaoke. It was clear where my fate lay.

The number ones had to dance to Tina Turner's "Nutbush City Limits," and I was so terrified at the prospect of "dancing" myself, that I can't even recall what the number threes were burdened with.

My eyes roamed the perimeter of the room, scanning the exits. I was also desperately searching my mind for an excuse not to take part. Needless to say, I can't dance to save my life and feel desperately self-conscious in the vicinity of a dance floor at the best of times. Let's just say the prospect of "strutting my stuff" in front of five hundred people was about as appealing to me as cage fighting.

The second round of the karaoke set was truly awful, and sure enough, the number fives would dance. Oh joy. Encouraged by my table colleagues, I walked onto the floor. I was sweating so much that I felt sure my feet would slip out of my shoes. Six of us lined up in front of the stage, as I stared at the floor. None of us knew what the music track would be, and I vowed that if the Chicken Dance struck up, I would be on my way to the airport before the votes were in.

Thank God for the Village People. I mean, even I can

dance to "Y.M.C.A." All I had to do was march up and down on the spot until the chorus kicked in and then give it all I had with the alphabet bit. While those first few bars thumped out of the speakers, I can't recall ever feeling so relieved. I marched with passion and purpose, defining each letter as if there were no tomorrow. As far as I was concerned, mine was a standout performance, and it was all I could do not to demand a recount when I wasn't presented with the trophy.

Chapter 43

Back in Town

I returned to the US and set about trying to achieve a balance between gardening and office work. I needed the gardening work to pay the rent, but by the same token, the more time and effort I could invest in recruiting franchisees the more likely it was the business would succeed.

I managed to retain most of my regular clients and granted myself the luxury of only doing one-off jobs for people that I liked (or at the very least found attractive) and who were prepared to pay whatever I quoted.

No disrespect to Mrs. Annett, but she didn't exactly check off all those boxes.

She was a nice old lady (half blind and largely deaf), who lived in Riverside. Her niece worked in the accounts department at SiteOne, and she had been let down and ripped off by any number of contractors in the past. I agreed to help her out as a favor, even though she contradicted pretty much every qualifying criterion I had recently set - with the sole exception of the fact she was single.

Her property was an absolute jungle. The grass was more than a foot long, the garden beds were hopelessly overgrown, and there were several hidden threats lurking throughout, in the shape of rusted sheets of iron, rocks, stones, and an abandoned shopping cart. The job didn't call for garden maintenance so much as guerrilla warfare.

Mrs. Annett wanted the garden beds tidied up and all the grass to be neatly mown. It was a task that had clearly chased off a few predecessors and one I simply didn't have the time to do. Still, I didn't want to let her down, so I proposed to come by each week and do what I could, until the lawns could sustain being mown every other week - a time frame that would realistically measure months. She seemed grateful that I was prepared to make any sort of commitment and kept me supplied with generous quantities of coffee and donuts throughout my tenure.

Mrs. Annett was one client who had her own catchphrase. She owned a small dog. It was yappy, small, fluffy, and white, and it barked and growled at every opportunity. It was impossible to say hello, accept a drink, or simply chat without Mrs. Annett taking time out to berate the little beast. Every exchange we ever had (no matter how brief) was invariably punctuated with cries of "Shuddup, Ginny!" Needless to say, each one didn't make the slightest difference.

Another client that managed to slip under the radar of my new selection regime was Gus and Linda Thorogood. They lived in a small cottage on Overlook Drive that adjoined a large orchard. Mrs. Thorogood worked with a shipping agent in New York, while her husband was retired, having spent several years working at the Australian Embassy. These days, Gus got around in an aging Volvo Estate, but in the past, he had driven a succession of diplomats to and from various appointments in something a bit grander.

The Thorogoods bred clumber spaniels for show, and they had one quite successful graduate in residence at the time. As far as I could tell, the clumber was a relatively obscure breed, and I believe quite an intelligent and perceptive one, since the whole time I worked there, it was clear their prized show dog would never forgive me for calling him "Bucket Head."

The dog had returned from a trip to the vet one day with a plastic cone strapped around his neck (hence the nickname), and I swear he took great offense to it. Up to that point, we had gotten along perfectly well, but thereafter, he growled and threatened me at every opportunity. It's a very sensitive breed the clumber.

Gus and I became great mates, and I took his incredible rudeness to be an indication of genuine affection. He derided and trashed the quality of my work at every opportunity, rolled his eyes at the prospect of making me a cup of coffee, and relished telling me that I "couldn't run a bath let alone a business."

In between insults, he showed me his workshop, where he handcrafted all manner of wooden implements and invited me inside the house to show me his various wartime naval memorabilia.

We spent as much time talking to one another as I ever

did working. I was often presented with a cup of coffee as soon as I arrived and then Gus and I would sit together in the garden. More than once, I had thanked him for the coffee, handed him my empty cup, and started to leave before realizing that I hadn't actually done any work.

Chapter 44

The Big Day Out

I had by now managed to free up a couple of days each week to spend in the office and to travel around the country. In the office, I enjoyed speaking with new customers on the phone and allocating job leads to franchisees on our computer system. It gave me a sense that the advertising we were coordinating was working, and it was very satisfying to see our franchisees deriving some benefit from all the work we were doing.

I was well and truly stumped one afternoon however, when a customer called the office having seen one of our ads in a local magazine. A gentleman wanted someone to come out and give him a quote to trim the hedge and mow the lawn.

"Certainly, sir," I responded, my fingers poised over the keyboard, ready to enter his address into the system. "We can help you with that," I said. "Tell me, whereabouts are you located?"

"I'm at home," he said.

The job was eventually allocated to Keith Davis who was an engineer from Vermont. He had driven down with his wife to meet with us at the office a couple of months before.

Meetings with prospective franchisees generally took about an hour or two. Keith's had taken four. To describe his preparation as thorough would be a massive understatement. He had studied our information literature and arrived with one hundred and forty questions typed on four legal-sized sheets of paper. Many were answered during the course of general conversation, and any that were not, we worked through on an individual basis. I considered it a great compliment to the Harry's system that after such a thorough investigation, Keith had decided to go ahead and invest in a franchise, and it came as no surprise when he continued to make a tremendous success of it.

We were anxious by this stage to gather all of our franchisees (and some of our more serious prospects) together in order to build a kind of team ethic among us all. We had people operating from Vermont to Virginia, and we were anxious to try and overcome the distances between us and draw everyone closer together.

I spoke with some friends from a local baseball club and managed to secure the use of their field, equipment, and clubhouse for the inaugural Harry's Big Day Out event. The idea was to invite family members and divide our franchisees into two teams, before staging a softball match, with an engraved trophy awarded to the winning captain. We booked a jumping castle and a barbecue, together with tables, chairs, ice, beer, wine, soft drinks, and salads.

What we needed was a roof.

Suffice to say, it rained on and off all day. We spent much of the time huddled together in the clubhouse, while I made the occasional dash to the beer tent, arguably providing the day's highlight, as I executed a spectacular back-flip, landing in a puddle adjacent to the barbecue.

Another initiative we developed was a horticultural training course that each and every new franchisee would have the opportunity to attend. Many of our recruits had brought little or no gardening knowledge with them, so we devised a three-day course in conjunction with a local horticultural college that was designed to give them a thorough (if relatively basic) induction and hopefully to provide a platform for further training. We were very lucky that the course was designed and presented by Stephen Harmes, one of the college's most experienced and likeable lecturers. What Stephen didn't know about horticulture and gardening wasn't worth knowing, but above all, his presentation style, and overall demeanor proved an ideal fit.

Since we had people travelling from all over the country, we agreed to put everyone up for two nights at a nearby hotel, which gave us all the opportunity to convene over dinner at a local restaurant. Everyone seemed to enjoy the events, and it gave some of our guys the opportunity to ask questions of Stephen in a more relaxed and social environment.

CHAPTER 45

NO ACCOUNTING FOR TASTE

As much as I enjoyed servicing my regular clients, to say nothing of the fact I needed the money, I had to step back from the practical side of things and focus on the business overall. We had taken over the operation of the call center, which meant we were taking dozens of phone calls from clients and prospective franchisees, and it was unfair to leave Cathy in the office on her own each day.

Andy Burns was one of our franchisees who had recently relocated to Connecticut when his father in law became ill, and he was able to take over all of my regulars in and around Greenwich. It was a bit of a commute from Norwalk, but he would have a ready-made client base and a decent supply of coffee and biscuits. He never thanked me for handing him Young and Nasty Mrs. Phillips as a client, but he did keep me updated with his various misadventures at "Squirrels," to say nothing of his ongoing campaign to get himself sacked.

To be fair, Andy probably suffered even more than me, as he bore witness to various altercations with the neighbors and numerous spats between the two. I recall receiving a text that he sent me one hot day, having been confronted in the garden by a braless Young Mrs. Phillips, wearing a skimpy tank top and a pair of pink hot pants that were hitched high above her waist. Andy described her outfit as like something out of *Baywatch*. The mental picture I had was more akin to *Nightmare on Elm Street*.

In the meantime, Michael Hughes was making great strides in Washington and anxious to develop his business further, he enrolled in an additional two day horticultural training course. He accepted an invitation to stay a couple of nights in my apartment and arrived with a plethora of goodies, some of which he had picked up during a recent holiday to Scotland. It consisted of a bottle of whisky, some delicious cheese, a packet of shortbread cookies, and a haggis - a traditional Scottish meat dish.

I put the whisky aside and devoured the cheese and cookies in no time at all, while the haggis stayed in the fridge for a while. I was never too sure just when I should cook it. I knew something of its reputation and that many considered it an acquired taste. I figured it was too risky to inflict on anyone else, so one Sunday evening I decided to treat myself.

All I really knew of Haggis was that whatever its contents, they were housed and subsequently cooked in a sheep's stomach. So were you supposed to eat the stomach as well or just the contents? I had no idea what was inside, since all that the label offered was a flag of St. Andrew crowning the word haggis, along with a sell-by date that was regrettably, some months in the future.

The one Michael had left me with was relatively small. It was about the size of a grapefruit and quite heavy. "Packed full of the flavor and spirit of the Highlands," I suspect. In any case, I peeled off the plastic wrapper and left it sitting in a saucepan full of boiling water, as per the instructions on the label.

Some twenty minutes later, I was sitting at the table, knife and fork in hand, staring at the steaming beige blob that I had just plonked on my plate. It could not have looked any less appealing, and I found it difficult to reconcile the fact that this was in fact "dinner," since it looked more like a tumor than a meal. I poked at it with a fork and made an initial incision with my knife. The skin was actually quite thin, and it came off easily enough, allowing a coarse, gray-colored mince to slowly ooze out. I cut it all the way across the top and from side to side, peeling the skin away to open the contents up completely. I was worried that it may not be cooked properly, so I picked through the mince with a fork, looking for any meat that was lighter or pink in color. The bland, gray texture was entirely consistent throughout however, liberally dosed as it was with hundreds of tiny white pods that looked to me like insect larvae.

There was nothing I could see that I particularly wanted to put in my mouth, let alone swallow, but in the interests of curiosity and the fact that Michael might one day ask, I gathered a small portion on the end of my fork, threw caution to the wind and introduced it to my tongue.

It tasted like soil.

Completely devoid of any discernible flavor or texture, it

was about as appealing as a spoonful of mud. In the interests of fair play, I tried a second, then a third portion. Each one smaller than the last and each one equally foul. I had clearly reached an impassable cultural divide and could go no further, but satisfied that I could now claim to have "eaten Haggis," I promptly threw the rest of it in the trash, rang the Lantern Chinese Restaurant for takeout, and ordered the King Prawn with Cashew Nuts.

Chapter 46

Beaten and Shot

We found ourselves particularly busy in the office throughout the spring and summer and took on a part-time employee, to help with all the phone calls and also to co-ordinate the local advertising for our growing number of franchisees.

Roma Thomas brought her black Labrador into the office each day and often regaled us with stories of her weekends hunting pheasants in New Hampshire. She travelled across the country, working as a "beater," which meant she and her dog would stroll around the countryside trying to flush defenseless birds out of the scrub, so that some clown with a shotgun could blast them out of the sky. I thought it sounded like great fun, and one day she arranged for me to come along.

We arrived at a property that was owned by a fellow called Iva, a man who fitted the country gent stereotype to a tee. He was an older man, bearded with gray hair, and a shotgun.

There were five or six "guns," all dressed exactly the same, in tweed sports jackets with leather patches, and as many beaters dressed more randomly, of which I was one.

Apparently the pheasants themselves were born and reared in pens before being released to feed on the remnants of recently harvested crops and whatever they could scrounge in the forest, until the onset of the shooting season. Just how many might survive into next year would largely depend on how good a shot Iva and his chums were.

The guns took up designated positions at the bottom of a hill or the end of a field, while the beaters and dogs would work their way toward them in a line, whooping, hollering, and wielding big sticks, as they tried to coax any birds nestling there up into the air.

Our first few runs were largely uneventful with barely a shot being fired, but it was still pleasant enough to wander between different sites, sipping all manner of concoctions from various hip flasks that others had brought along.

We hadn't managed to bag many birds to date but soon stumbled on an area where the pheasants seemed to have gathered in greater numbers. I hadn't seen a single bird all day, but as I bashed my way through the undergrowth, I could see a large male pecking at the ground a few feet in front of me. There were no other beaters or dogs near me at the time, and I decided that this would indeed be "my bird." I ran toward it, crashing through the scrub, waving my arms about and making as much noise as I could. It certainly had the desired effect. This pheasant wasn't sticking around. He took to the air and flew directly away from me, right into the path of the guns. Perfect!

I shouted "Forward!" as loudly as I could, watching that handsome plump bird silhouetted against a bright blue sky. A deafening shot rang out just ahead of me, followed by another, as the bird flew on and on into the distance.

I didn't bother to conceal my disappointment and trudged forward, yelling, "You bloody great pelican!" Hoping to deride and embarrass the sheer incompetent who had missed such a gilt-edged opportunity. I didn't realize the "gun" in question was close enough to actually hear what I had said, nor did I realize who it was until I brushed past a couple of large shrubs.

Disappointment was etched across his face, his still smoking gun cradled in his arms.

"Bad luck, Iva," I said. "Perhaps we'll get him next year."

It was probably just as well he had fired off both cartridges.

I had to leave the shoot early, not for fear of Iva's retribution but because another of Roma's friends had arranged for me to take part in an "Introduction to Business" workshop at a local high school the next day. My task was to give a short presentation to groups of fifteen-year-old schoolgirls, outlining the structure of Harry's Landscaping and what exactly constitutes a franchise. I had prepared a PowerPoint presentation that explained the company's origins and ethos, before detailing its system of fees, territory, and work allocation.

The first group was herded into a classroom at 10:00 a.m., and soon afterward, they were introduced to all things

Harry's. Twenty minutes, and not a single question later, they were ushered out again, with the exception of one girl who had incurred the wrath of her teacher. I didn't know what she had done but she was clearly in serious trouble. After much finger-pointing and gnashing of teeth, the teacher directed the child toward me, demanding she apologize. I had no idea what had occurred and felt quite embarrassed for her. As far as I could recall, no one had misbehaved during the presentation, and it's not as if I was struck by any flying objects throughout.

"I'm really sorry," she said sheepishly, her chin resting against her chest. "I'm just really tired."

I looked up at the clock on the wall. It was twenty past ten.

"That's all right," I said. "Don't worry about it," then laughing, I added "You didn't fall asleep, did you?"

"Yes," she said.

I was crushed.

I didn't expect to be mobbed afterward, much less signing autographs, but how more boring could my presentation have been?! In just twenty minutes, I had transformed a bright, intelligent, healthy adolescent into a narcoleptic.

I shuffled into the staff room and slouched on a couch in the company of some of the other presenters. I confessed my crime, along with the fact that I now just wanted to go home. Some bloke from Microsoft coached and cajoled me. He assured me that these were indeed very bright and clever kids, and that they would not respond to simply being lectured to. What I needed to do was give them a task, a project they could work through that might stimulate their minds.

Emboldened, I returned to the fray and gave the next group the task of developing an advertising concept that we might use as a poster or print ad to recruit new franchisees. I divided the class into groups of four, and gave them each ten minutes to develop and sketch an idea.

The results were outstanding. Some groups developed ideas that contrasted city landscapes with urban greenery and outcomes that promised a more attractive lifestyle. One idea was even better than the recruitment concept we ourselves had developed and were currently using. Our concept featured a Harry's franchisee sitting on a riding mower, beneath a headline that read "How do you commute to work?" The concept that emanated from a handful of schoolgirls, showed a group of unhappy, frustrated commuters sitting on a train, seemingly unaware that behind them, through the windows of the train, we could see the lifestyle opportunity that a Harry's franchise represents. Franchisees could be seen mowing lawns, pruning shrubs, and trimming hedges. The sky was blue, the grass was green, and the sun was shining. What's more, the picture of the unhappy commuters in the foreground would appear in black and white. Above it all, a headline read "Where would you rather be?"

I thought it was absolutely brilliant and as clever and thoughtful a concept as the most experienced creative team in a top New York ad agency would have come up with. At the time, Beth, Izzy, Katie, and Louisa were fifteen-year-old schoolgirls.

I predicted a very bright future for them all.

Chapter 47

Virginia

Relationships and business partnerships can be difficult to maintain at the best of times and ours was certainly no different.

My new business partner and I had been thrust together when Jason returned to Australia, more out of necessity than through any careful planning or consideration. In hindsight, it was destined never to work.

My partner had insisted that we relocate our office to Virginia, and a few months later, we were ensconced in what was once a stately home near Richmond, that had been converted into offices. Roma and I were commuting from Connecticut and staying two nights a week in a hotel, while Cathy managed to secure a new job not far from where we were originally located. We were of course still obliged to answer phone calls and allocate job leads to our franchisees. To help us, we employed a recent high school graduate for a few months before she started college.

Sophie was tall, blonde, and athletic. She was eighteen

years old and seemed to think that hiding behind the fridge and suddenly leaping out at people (all but instigating a massive heart attack), was a perfectly reasonable way to pass the time on a slow afternoon.

I was probably lucky to survive that day at all, since I was later called upon to demonstrate how our battery operated "fly zapping tennis racket" worked.

"It's quite simple," I said, demonstrating my forehand. "You just push the button here and whack the little beast like so," tapping the head of the racket against the ball of my thumb.

"Why doesn't that hurt your hand?" Sophie asked.

"Well, it's got these wires running across it," I said, pointing with my finger. "The fly itself slips through…"

There was a sticker attached to the racket that read "This is not a toy." I wish it was bigger. I might have noticed it. I might have read it, and I might even have paid attention to it. Lest anyone be in any doubt, two AA-size batteries connected to a wire mesh (that was designed to electrocute small insects), can still pack one hell of a punch. At least they do when you stick the tip of your index finger in there.

I continued to commute from Greenwich for a couple of months, before I rented an apartment that was close to the office, on the outskirts of a suburb called Wyndham.

I often wondered why we had relocated to Virginia at all, given my partner came into the office for at best, a couple of hours a week. On the few occasions that he did come in, he would greet me, while completely ignoring people like Roma and Sophie.

When I spoke to him about it, suggesting that perhaps he didn't realize just how rude he was being, he replied, "Why should I talk to them? They're just the staff."

Chapter 48

The Last Chapter

I don't think I will ever forget the day I was driving north out of Richmond, when the phone rang. I pulled over and spoke with one of our local operators who had purchased a franchise from my business partner a couple of years before.

He asked me, "Why can't I have a territory closer to where I live?"

I was confused by his question, as we had always allocated franchisees a territory exactly where they lived. Working close to home only served to reduce travel time, but this fellow was travelling fifteen miles from his home every working day, just to reach the outskirts of his own territory. It didn't make any sense.

I called him back, as soon as I arrived in the office the next day. As we spoke, it soon dawned on me what had happened. My business partner had sold this fellow a franchise, allocating him a territory within his own region. That meant that my partner alone would secure the entire franchise sale proceeds and ongoing fees. Had this fellow been allocated a territory near his home (which was well outside of my partner's own region), his sale and fee income would have been directed to our company.

I drafted an email to my business partner, since there was a good chance we wouldn't see him for at least a week, and explained the content of my telephone conversations with our franchisee. I asked him to explain what had happened and why. I didn't accuse him of anything, despite some overwhelming evidence, and suggested that allocating a territory to a franchisee some fifteen miles from his home was "surely not in anyone's best interests."

The following day, I received an email in reply. It was littered with every derogatory and critical adjective imaginable. Apparently, I was extremely rude, grossly offensive, disingenuous, disloyal, and arrogant. My behavior was appalling, shameful, disrespectful, and the list went on. It ended with some rather nasty physical threats.

I sent the following message in reply;

"Did you get a thesaurus for your birthday?"

In Australian parlance, I was clearly dealing with someone who had "a couple of kangaroos loose in the top paddock," and in hindsight, the thesaurus jibe probably wasn't a very smart play.

Early one morning the following week, there was a knock at the door of my apartment in Wyndham. I opened it to see my business partner standing with a uniformed security guard. He handed me an envelope and said, "I'm sorry, but you leave me no choice," and left.

The envelope contained a letter. Apparently, I was guilty

of gross misconduct. My employment and directorship had been terminated with immediate effect, just as the car I had been driving was being towed away. What's more, my computer had been confiscated, and the office locks had been changed. Any attempt to enter the office building would be considered trespassing.

Roma was at home in Connecticut when all of this had happened, and she had the good sense to stay there, while Sophie decided to leave right then and there, but not before she arranged to divert all incoming office calls to my cell phone.

Thereafter, I took up residence in the Wyndham Library, answering phone calls and allocating job leads to our franchisees on the Internet. I wasn't sure to what degree any of them were even aware of what had happened, and I thought it best to just keep things moving along as best I could, for the time being at least.

Soon after, Roma was kind enough to drive down and pick me up from Virginia, extending an invitation to stay at her house, from where I was able to make an appointment with our accountant Bob Lawrence.

By this point, word had spread throughout the franchise network, and I had to endure several angry phone calls and one or two face-to-face meetings with franchisees, who were understandably very upset and concerned about their investment.

In each instance, I tried to explain that it simply wasn't realistic to have two people in charge who were (to all intents and purposes), at war with one another, and I thought it would be best for everyone if I could find a way to move on.

After all, as my business partner was so fond of reminding me, I was "just a minority shareholder," now with no car and no income.

As angry and upset as I was at what had happened to me, I still tried to reassure our franchisees that what mattered most was the brand, the systems, and the territory or region that they had invested in, and all of that was far greater and more valuable than anything any one individual could bring to the equation. None of them seemed the least bit convinced, which was very disappointing, and I promised to do all I could to remedy the situation.

Before meeting with Bob, I placed a call to the Harry's head office in Australia. I explained everything in great detail, what had transpired and everything that I was trying to do to hold things together. I said that my foremost priorities were the interests and welfare of our franchisees and that we had to be careful, lest the reputation and standing of the brand and business in the US was to suffer.

But my "cry for help" was met with quite staggering indifference.

I sat in a chair with the phone pressed against my ear, and it was some time before I had the presence of mind to actually hang up. I dare say everyone that I had just spoken with had already been presented with a vastly different version of events.

By this point, I had pretty much run out of options. I had no desire to try and repair the relationship with my business partner, but all the same, I wasn't prepared to see everything I had worked so hard for go to waste. Later that day, I sent him an email. I explained that our differences were "clearly irreconcilable," and I suggested that perhaps our accountant could broker an arrangement whereby one of us could buy the other's share of the business. I explained that calls to the office had been diverted to my cell phone and that I would continue allocating job leads to our franchisees. Fortunately, franchise inquiries almost always came to us via email, so I left him to deal with that element.

Roma very kindly and very generously said that I could stay with her for as long as I needed, so I emailed my Wyndham landlord. I drafted a brief explanation, apologized and suggested he keep my security deposit.

For the next couple of months, I set up camp in Roma's house. I slept in her spare room and established a makeshift office downstairs, just behind the kitchen, as Bob Lawrence continued to liaise with my nemesis. I didn't have the means or capacity to take over the entire business myself and given what had transpired, I didn't particularly want to.

About ten weeks later, a degree of common sense eventually prevailed, and I sold my share of the business to my now former partner. Perhaps that was his plan all along, but it was a bittersweet moment. I was certainly grateful and relieved to put the whole episode behind me, but I felt terribly conflicted, having abandoned the ship, leaving our franchisees to their own fate. All the same, everyone would surely be better off without suffering through the civil war that had broken out, and someone had to step aside, if only to make the peace. In this case, it just happened to me.

It was a great shame that things ended how they did, but I still believe that my whole foray into the US was indeed a grand adventure.

Things may not have worked out as well as I had hoped, but I don't regret setting out on the journey that I did for a second.

Above all, I had a tremendous time living in America.

It is a wonderful country, populated by friendly, generous people, and one that boasts an extraordinary and rich history.

I had really enjoyed my recruitment role in particular, and I had developed some wonderful relationships with customers, franchisees, suppliers, and staff along the way. I had come to consider many of these people my friends, and I was already looking forward to seeing some of them again.

After ten years in the United States, I returned to Australia in February, 2011. I was sad to leave, but by the same token, I wouldn't miss being mauled by psychotic dogs, attacked by stinging nettles and being abused by angry old women.

As we flew at thirty thousand feet, somewhere over the Pacific, I can remember thinking to myself, "I just might write a book about all this."

How hard could it be…?

A Note from the Author

Thank you for reading my book *Yards and Stripes*. It really is very humbling to think that someone would invest the time to read something that I have written.

I hope you enjoyed it, and if you did, perhaps you would be kind enough to draft a short review on the website where you bought it? It doesn't have to be much. Just a few words would be great. It all helps.

Many thanks
Michael Francis

www.ingramcontent.com/pod-product-compliance
Lightning Source LLC
Chambersburg PA
CBHW070253010526
44107CB00056B/2443